FIRESIDE

# ✓CHECKLISTS
## Everyone's Guide to Getting Things Done

## Carol Nichols and Jan Lurie

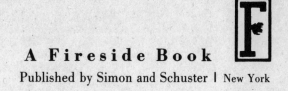

A Fireside Book
Published by Simon and Schuster | New York

A Fireside Book
Published by Simon and Schuster
A Division of Gulf & Western Corporation
Simon & Schuster Building
Rockefeller Center
1230 Avenue of the Americas
New York, New York 10020

FIRESIDE and colophon are trademarks of Simon & Schuster.
Designed by Irving Perkins Associates
Manufactured in the United States of America
Printed and bound by The Murray Printing Co.

1 2 3 4 5 6 7 8 9 10

Library of Congress Cataloging in Publication Data
Nichols, Carol.
Checklists, everyone's guide to getting things done.

(A Fireside book)
Includes index.
1. Handbooks, vade-mecums, etc.   I. Lurie, Jan.
II. Title
AG105.N58 1982          031'.02          81-9118
AACR2
ISBN 0-671-41460-7

*To Saul, Steve, and Amy, my staunchest supporters,*
*who endured through it all*
*. . . C.N.*

*To Sherm, Josh, Liz, and Joe, whose hugs are*
*always with me*
*. . . J.L.*

# Acknowledgments

The authors gratefully wish to acknowledge the assistance of many individuals who took time to share their expertise with us: Irma Davis, Director of Therapeutic Recreational Services, New York University Medical Center; Susan Dower, Health Insurance Institute; Doris Handy and George Lenz, Insurance Information Institute; Carmen Cappadona, Civil Aeronautics Board; V. J. Bileris, Pan Am World Airways, Inc.; Beatrice Mite, U.S. Passport Agency; LaVerne Drayton Bey, Bank Street Day Care Consultation Center; Allan Stolz, American Camping Association; Bonnie Shapiro, Assistant Superintendent of Chester, N.Y., School District; Lloyd Feinstein, Personnel Director and Manny Cordova, Benefits Coordinator, Cadence Industries, Inc.; Renee Leonard, ASID; Milt Dobkin, President of Chematic Systems, Inc.; Steve Lapidus, J. D., Real Estate Institute, New York University.

We would like to give credit to the following for their permission to adapt previously published material: *Annual Educational Checkup*, copyright © 1978, National Committee for Citizens in Education, Columbia, MD; *Retirement and the Law*, by *50 Plus* Magazine, copyright © 1980, Retirement Living Publishing Co.

The authors would also like to acknowledge those organizations that contributed invaluable source material: Bank of America; Benjamin Moore & Co.; American Veterinary Medical Association; Aviation Consumer Action Project; Camp Trails, Division of Johnson Camping, Inc.; New York State Office of Crime Prevention; Aero-Mayflower Transit Company, Inc.; American Health Care Association; U.S. Small Business Administration; U.S. Department of Housing and Urban Development.

We would also like to thank those who encouraged us with their personal support and their invaluable advice: Ron Derven, John Miller, Allan Legon, Hazel Weinberg, Robert Sillins, Phyllis and Robert Finkelstein, George and Gert Rosenberg, Gerry Youcha, Jack Galub, Bea and Ben Laitin, and Connie Clausen.

# Contents

# Your Household 97

# Your Car 119

# Your Children 133

# Your Health 161

# Personal Matters 177

# Index 209

# Foreword

*Checklists* grew out of our experiences. For years before we ever thought of writing the book, we were accomplished list makers. And, as we began to discuss the idea of the book with people we knew, we found that *they* were list makers too. Men, women, young people, old people—everyone makes lists.

Once we had systematically developed the kinds of lists that would organize our own lives most efficiently, we decided to expand the book to include lists designed to help in making major decisions—things like what to consider before buying into a co-op and how to go about choosing a college. At that point we had to do extensive research and to conduct interviews with a series of experts. Lawyers, car mechanics, college admissions advisors and many other valuable sources gave us a great deal of information, which we have pared down for fast, useful reference.

Our purpose is to provide you with a comprehensive and well-organized list for every one of those activities about which you say, "Next time I'm going to get organized. Next time I'm going to make a list." Now you have it.

# When You Travel

- ☐ **Things to Do When Luggage Is Lost**

- ☐ **Basic Vacation Packing List**

- ☐ **Business Trip Checklist**

- ☐ **Overseas Travel Checklist**

- ☐ **Outdoor Camping List**

- ☐ **Checklist for Car Travel with Kids**

- ☐ **Vacation Packing List for Children**

- ☐ **First Aid Supply List for Camping**

- ☐ **Checklist for Traveling with Pets**

- ☐ **Before-You-Go-on-Vacation List**

# ✓ Things to Do When Luggage Is Lost

□ Act fast when luggage does not appear on conveyor belt; notify airline personnel to check if it is still on plane.

□ See baggage service representative to fill out Property Irregularity report before leaving airport; note temporary address and phone number as well as permanent one.

□ Get airline official's signature on this report; retain a signed copy of this, your passenger ticket coupon and baggage claim check(s).

□ Ask rep for baggage claim form; try to avoid having it mailed to you. (This is to be filled out at home.)

□ See supervisor or customer service rep at airport and ask about advance money to replace necessities. (You may be refused; there is no standard policy. It's up to you to negotiate given circumstances such as being away from home or without a business suit for meetings.)

□ Keep a record of all expenses incurred in connection with lost luggage and names of airline employees you deal with in person or on the phone.

□ On reaching destination, call airline Lost and Found frequently; give hotel room number, itinerary changes. Go there and look through piles of luggage yourself if schedule permits.

□ After you arrive home, fill out the baggage claim form; read the fine print. (This form is used to evaluate your claim.)

□ Send airline claims department photocopies of supporting documents, retaining originals for your records:

___ passenger ticket coupon
___ baggage claim check(s)
___ Property Irregularity report (second copy)
___ proof of value for items claimed (sales slips, cancelled checks, etc.)
___ receipts for out-of-pocket expenses
___ inventory list of bag contents
___ baggage claim form

□ Write short letters expressing your concern if weeks go by without a response; keep copies. If no settlement comes through from domestic airline after two months, write that you intend to contact your lawyer.

□ Refrain from cashing any check that airline sends if you think compensation is unreasonably low to cover your loss.

□ Write again, explaining what you expect in the way of reimbursement; indicate if you plan to go to small-claims court or take other legal action.

□ Pull copies of all previous correspondence with airline from your file; send to organizations that will review your case.

___ Bureau of Consumer Protection at the Civil Aeronautics Board (or one of the field offices)
Washington, D. C. 20428
___ Aviation Consumer Action Project
P. O. Box 19029
Washington, D. C. 20036

## *Things to Remember*

- Airline tariff rules limit their liability for checked baggage; if any part of your trip involved international travel international rules would apply and the settlement process takes longer.

- Reimbursement policy is based on airline's estimate of the depreciated value of your lost possessions, not replacement costs.

- Although you have forty-five days to make a written claim, the sooner you go on record, and the more often you show concern, the stronger your claim looks to the airline.

- Notify your own insurance company if your homeowner's policy covers loss of personal effects outside home, or if you took out special trip insurance. Find out if it pays before collection from airline, or if you have to collect from airline first with your insurance company making up the difference.

# Basic Vacation Packing List

**Outerwear**

☐ coat

   ___ topcoat
   ___ all-purpose coat
   ___ raincoat
   ___ casual coat
   ___ _____

☐ suit(s)

   ___ _____
   ___ _____

☐ slacks

   ___ sport
   ___ dress
   ___ jeans
   ___ _____
   ___ _____

☐ jackets

   ___ sports
   ___ dress
   ___ _____
   ___ _____

☐ sweaters

   ___ heavy
   ___ light
   ___ sleeveless
   ___ shawl
   ___ _____

☐ dresses

   ___ sports
   ___ dressy
   ___ _____

☐ skirts

   ___ long
   ___ informal
   ___ _____

☐ blouses/tops

   ___ casual
   ___ dress
   ___ _____

☐ shirts

   ___ long sleeves/sports
   ___ short sleeves
   ___ dress
   ___ _____

**Underwear/sleepwear**

☐ shorts

☐ undershirts

☐ socks

   ___ sports
   ___ dress
   ___ high
   ___ _____

☐ stockings

☐ bras

☐ panties/girdle

☐ slips

☐ pajamas/nightgown

☐ bathrobe

☐ slippers

**Footwear**

☐ shoes/extra laces

   ___ walking
   ___ casual
   ___ sandals
   ___ dress sandals
   ___ evening shoes
   ___ boots
   ___ rainshoes/rubbers
   ___ _____

**Toiletries**

☐ toothbrush/toothpaste/dental floss

☐ brush and comb

☐ shampoo/shower cap

☐ deodorant

☐ soap and container

☐ razor and blades

☐ shaving cream

☐ towel/washcloth

☐ talcum powder

☐ handcream/moisturizer

☐ facial tissues/towelettes

☐ cotton swabs

☐ make-up

   ___ eye shadow
   ___ mascara
   ___ lipstick
   ___ eye liner
   ___ face powder
   ___ _____
   ___ _____
   ___ _____
   ___ _____

☐ sanitary supplies

☐ hair: blowdryer/electric rollers

☐ manicure kit

   ___ nail scissors
   ___ emery board
   ___ polish/remover
   ___ cuticle nipper

☐ sewing kit

    ___ needles
    ___ thread
    ___ pins
    ___ buttons
    ___ _____
    ___ _____

☐ spot removers

☐ transparent tape

☐ traveling clothesline

☐ plastic clothespins

☐ all-purpose scissors

☐ shoeshine applicators

☐ _____

## Medical

☐ insurance card/numbers

☐ prescriptions

☐ extra glasses/prescription

☐ sunglasses

☐ motion sickness pills

☐ antihistamine/nasal decongestant/laxative

☐ salt tablets

☐ vitamins

☐ petroleum jelly

☐ Band-Aids

☐ antacid

☐ sunburn lotion

☐ aspirin

☐ _____

## Accessories

☐ hat

    ___ sport
    ___ dress
    ___ rain
    ___ _____
    ___ _____

☐ belts

    ___ dress
    ___ sport
    ___ _____

☐ ties

☐ handkerchiefs

☐ scarf

☐ gloves

☐ handbags

    ___ sports
    ___ dress

☐ wallet

☐ jewelry

    ___ watch
    ___ tie tack
    ___ necklace
    ___ _____
    ___ _____
    ___ _____
    ___ _____

## Special Weather Items

☐ bathing suit/trunks/cap

☐ beach robe/jacket

☐ shorts
    ___ Bermuda
    ___ tennis
    ___ _____

☐ beach towel

☐ insect repellent

☐ ski pants

☐ parka

☐ ski hat/mask/mittens

☐ après-ski boots

☐ sports gear

    ___ tennis racket
    ___ skis
    ___ _____
    ___ _____
    ___ _____
    ___ _____

☐ _____

☐ _____

☐ _____

## Miscellaneous

☐ plastic bags

☐ travel-alarm clock

☐ travel umbrella

☐ corkscrew/can opener

☐ stationery/pen/stamps

☐ camera/film/flash

☐ binoculars

☐ magnifying glass

☐ nature guidebook/maps

☐ _____

☐ _____

☐ _____

# ✔ Business Trip Checklist

## Financial Arrangements

☐ Find out company/client travel policy on where to stay, how to get there. Ask about:

___ prearrangements with travel agent, hotel chain, car rental agency
___ reservations on a guaranteed arrival basis
___ business discount rates
___ insurance coverage
___ _____

☐ Clarify recordkeeping required for reimbursement and legitimate business expenses:

___ entertainment
___ meals
___ gas mileage allowance
___ car rental/repairs
___ taxis/limousine
___ _____
___ _____

☐ Check IRS guidelines on business travel:

___ allowables on expenses not covered by company
___ limits on flight class
___ attendance at overseas conventions
___ required form of records
___ _____
___ _____

☐ Notify payroll department if you will be away when your paycheck is due; request advance if needed.

☐ Get traveler's checks and list numbers on separate sheet.

## Travel Arrangements

☐ Have travel agent book preferred flight (direct/stopover; night/day) and seat; work out connecting flights at the same time and have tickets forwarded to you in advance.

☐ Order taxi/limo for trip to airport.

☐ Reserve accommodations/facilities you require; get hotel confirmation in writing:

___ centrally located hotel/motel
___ office-type suite to receive business contacts
___ conference room for meetings
___ secretarial/translation services
___ catered luncheon/dinners
___ hotel dining room
___ car rental
___ _____

☐ If bound for Europe, find out about transcontinental train service between major business centers (with conference compartments and multilingual secretaries).

## Office Arrangements

☐ Prepare for shipment of bulk materials for convention/conferences; keep inventory list with you. Check:
___ special packing/handling
___ advance shipment/excess baggage on your flight
___ duty liability of sample merchandise
___ special delivery instructions/addresses
___ _____

□ Review upcoming office workload; reschedule appointments; leave detailed written instructions and take a copy with you; notify pertinent people of needed follow-ups.

□ Plan to take a typed list of daily scheduled meetings. Note who will be there, where you will be going. Include names of contacts, home and business telephone numbers and addresses you will need while on the road. Leave a copy at the office.

□ Prepare a packet of papers/reading material for plane if you want to use trip to catch up or get ahead on work.

## Take-along Items

___ large envelopes/stamps
___ manila folders
___ tape recorder/cassettes
___ pocket calculator
___ travel typewriter
___ pads/pencils/pens
___ travel-alarm clock
___ business papers/contracts
___ appointment book

___ expense report sheets
___ credit cards
___ traveler's checks/cash
___ driver's license
___ telephone numbers/addresses
___ club membership cards
___ _____
___ _____
___ _____

### *For a Smoother Trip*

□ Pack to carry off what you carry on. This often includes a hanging garment bag.

□ Keep dollar bills and change handy . . . take more money than you think you'll need . . . keep photocopies of credit cards apart from originals . . . carry checks, tickets, important papers separate from wallet.

□ Plan for leisure time . . . know hotel's recreational setup (sauna/pool/golf/tennis) . . . bring leisure reading and recreation gear (swim suit, jogging shoes).

□ Find out about visiting city . . . reciprocal club member privileges . . . fastest routes to business district . . . good restaurants.

□ Minimize jet lag by keeping as close to home schedule as possible . . . to bed early if flying west, late if going east.

□ Ask colleagues, foreign reps or tourist office about ways of doing business in foreign country . . . what items can be legally exported . . . which clubs might be useful to join for nonresidents.

□ Allow extra time for completing immigration and customs formalities.

□ Call airport just before leaving to see if flight is on time . . . check office for last-minute messages or instructions.

# Overseas Travel Checklist

## Take-alongs

- ☐ valid passport
- ☐ visas/tourist card
- ☐ international driver's license
- ☐ extra passport photos/expired passport
- ☐ currency

    ___ foreign      ___ change
    ___ U. S.      ___ traveler's checks
    ___ dollar bills      ___ credit cards

- ☐ pocket currency converter
- ☐ money clip/small wallet
- ☐ pocket metric converter/tape measure
- ☐ current adapters
- ☐ extension cord
- ☐ immersion coil
- ☐ pocket dictionary/phrase book/guidebook
- ☐ telephone-address book
- ☐ sleep shade/ear plugs
- ☐ toilet paper roll
- ☐ soap and container
- ☐ packets cold-water detergent
- ☐ disposable razor/European shaver
- ☐ antacid
- ☐ pocket flashlight/batteries
- ☐ camera/film/batteries
- ☐ cigarettes
- ☐ plastic shopping bag

___ _____

___ _____

___ _____

## Travel Documents

- • You will need a *valid passport* (it is valid for five years from issue date).

  - ☐ Fill out application at nearest U. S. passport agency, designated post office or court for a first passport; otherwise, call to find out if you are eligible to apply by mail.

  - ☐ Bring fifteen dollars to cover current fee; remit ten dollars if eligible to apply by mail.

  - ☐ To prove identity, bring a previous passport, your driver's license, a government or an employee's I.D. card.

  - ☐ To prove citizenship, bring a certified copy of your birth certificate or a previous passport.

  - ☐ If born abroad, bring your Certificate of Naturalization or Certificate of Citizenship or your previous U.S. passport.

  - ☐ Bring two identical photos (2″×2″ full face) taken within the past six months. Make extras in case you need an international driver's license or other documents while overseas.

  - ☐ Allow at least two weeks for processing application unless you have proof of urgent departure (airline ticket).

- • You may need *visas* or *tourist cards.*

  - ☐ Check with local consulates, airline or travel agency.

- • You may need *health certificates.*

  - ☐ Check local or state Public Health offices and the embassy or consulate of each country you plan to visit.

  - ☐ Have required vaccinations recorded on the International Certificates of Vaccination form.

☐ Get a doctor's certificate if you have to take medicines with a habit-forming or narcotic drug with you.

• You may need an *international driver's license.*

☐ Go to local AAA office for license.

☐ Bring two passport-type photos and your valid state license.

☐ Double-check restrictions on international license.

## Find Out

☐ *Will you be crossing the International Date Line?* Account for time differentials in making your various reservations.

☐ *Does your luggage conform to airline restrictions?* For Western Europe specific dimensions apply; beyond, most countries use weight as the standard; check latest rulings with airline.

☐ *Do your present insurance policies cover you while abroad?* Look over your homeowner/car/medical/accident policies. Consider trip insurance for yourself and belongings; ask about excess valuation at check-in time. (It increases airline liability in case of luggage damage or loss.)

☐ *What is the amount of local currency you can bring into or take out of the countries you will be visiting?* Check with a bank, foreign exchange firm, embassy or consulate before you leave. Buy enough to get you through the first day in a new country.

☐ *Have you planned your trip to take advantage of the latest special rates?* Check airlines and travel agent for information on the most current special rail passes, car rentals, event admissions, air fares that may be purchased here at a better price.

## For a Smoother Trip

• Allow time to register two-year-old-or-newer camera, watch or other foreign-made personal items at U. S. airport customs before departure.

• Expedite re-entry by keeping certificates and bills of sale for all articles acquired abroad in one place.

• Declare all gifts you take overseas as personal property.

• Keep your passport in your possession at all times; do not pack it in your luggage or carry-on bag.

• Pack only what you can carry yourself. Keep local customs in mind.

• Take valuables, one change of outfit, perishables, prescription medicines in carry-on luggage. Know generic names of prescriptions for refills.

• Remove all old destination tags ... distinguish your bag on the outside for easier identification and also attach I.D. tag ... place identifying label on inside as well.

• Keep inventory list of luggage contents with you.

• If you change planes, try to reclaim your bags yourself; check through again for next flight to lessen chance of lost luggage.

• Keep duplicate of traveler's-check numbers separate from checks.

• Leave detailed itinerary, including your passport number, with relatives, friend, business associates so you can be reached easily ... receive mail ... get money transferred quickly.

# ✓ Outdoor Camping List

What you take will vary depending on length and type of trip, season, your experience. (First-timers may want to borrow or rent most of the gear.)

## Backpacker Essentials (under 30 pounds)

☐ Shelter

- ____ tent/poles/fly tarp/stakes
- ____ sleeping bag (down or synthetic fiber-filled)
- ____ foam pad
- ____ ground cloth
- ____ braided nylon cord (100 feet)
- ____ camp ax
- ____ lantern/candles
- ____ _____
- ____ _____

☐ Cooking Equipment

- ____ camp stove/fuel cartridge or bottle/fire-starter tablets
- ____ fry pan
- ____ nesting pots
- ____ pot holders
- ____ pocketknife (Swiss Army type including can opener)
- ____ long utensils (tongs/spatula/tablespoon)
- ____ light tin plate/nesting fork/spoon
- ____ plastic bowl/nesting cup
- ____ canteens
- ____ collapsible plastic water container
- ____ heavy foil
- ____ biodegradable soap
- ____ pot scouring/scrub sponges
- ____ heavy-duty plastic bags/rubber bands
- ____ plastic wide-mouth jars
- ____ _____
- ____ _____

☐ Food

- ____ dehydrated/freeze-dried foods
- ____ salt/pepper
- ____ condiment tubes/soy sauce packets
- ____ cooking oil
- ____ powdered milk/drink mixes
- ____ coffee/tea/cocoa/sugar
- ____ pancake/biscuit mix/instant oatmeal
- ____ syrup/honey/jelly packets
- ____ peanut butter squeeze tubes
- ____ soup envelopes
- ____
- ____ trail snacks (chocolate/nuts/dried fruits/candy bars/gorp)
- ____ protein (powdered eggs/slab bacon/hard salami/pepperoni/cheese)
- ____ hard bread/pita bread
- ____ vitamins
- ____ _____
- ____ _____

☐ Clothing

- ____ hiking boots (your own)
- ____ socks (wool and liners)
- ____ underwear
- ____ hat/cap/bandanna
- ____ Windbreaker
- ____ poncho/gaiters
- ____ shirts (light/warm)
- ____ long pants
- ____ sweater (wool)
- ____ pajama or thermal underwear
- ____ down jacket/hood/gloves
- ____ swim suit
- ____ _____
- ____ _____

☐ Toiletries

- ____ wash basin
- ____ biodegradable soap/container
- ____ toilet paper
- ____ sanitary supplies
- ____ toothbrush/paste
- ____ towel

_____ comb/brush
_____ razor/blades
_____ mirror

_____ _____

_____ _____

☐ Miscellaneous Necessities

_____ lightweight pack and frame
_____ first-aid kit*
_____ matches in watertight container
_____ repair kit (extra shoelaces/strong thread

*See "First Aid Supply List for Camping" (page 28).

and needles/self-sticking repair tape/
tube of contact cement)
_____ flashlight/batteries
_____ insect repellent
_____ ground/air signals
_____ trowel
_____ compass/trail area map
_____ sunglasses
_____ watch
_____ coins for emergency calls
_____ fire permit/hunting/fishing license

_____ _____

_____ _____

## Mobile Camping Take-alongs

- folding chairs/table
- sheets/blankets/pillows
- clothespins/towels/washcloths
- cold-water detergent/laundry bag
- dish drainer/dishpan/towel
- sponges
- garbage can/bags
- fly swatter
- cooler/portable refrigerator
- portable barbecue stove/charcoal
- trenching shovel
- fire extinguisher
- plastic buckets
- propane lanterns/liquid-fuel canisters
- water storage container
- tablecloth
- paper plates/cups/napkins
- dishes/cups/flatware
- cutting board
- kitchen utensils
- Dutch oven
- coffeepot
- fry pan
- pots
- thermos
- canned meats/fish
- canned soups/vegetables

- canned milk
- onions
- potatoes
- eggs
- ketchup/mayonnaise/mustard
- peanut butter
- crackers/cookies
- bread
- butter/margarine
- screwdrivers/pliers
- hammer/nails
- jacksaw
- binoculars
- cards/games
- camera/film
- nature guide
- note pad and pencil
- fishing rod

## Your Favorite Camping Menus

- 
- 
- 
- 
- 
-

# Checklist for Car Travel with Kids

**Travel Plans**

☐ Contact national/state tourist offices/local chamber of commerce/travel agent. Find out:

___ dates of local events
___ special attractions for children
___ suitable family accommodations
  • near to shopping/restaurants/laundry
  • away from highway
  • playground nearby
  • housekeeping basics included in rental
  • other children in area
  • walking distance to pool/movies/kids' activities
  • availability of supervised play groups/ babysitters

☐ Involve children. Have them:

___ write for materials
___ read up on region
___ help decide what to see and do
___ discuss rules of behavior for travel
___ look at itinerary beforehand
___ find pen pals to visit
___ bone up on quiet car games

☐ Contact AAA:

___ get current road maps
___ outline car route
___ check gas stations/availability
___ plan stops of interest/family side trips
___ recommended hotels/motels for families

**Checkups**

☐ Bring car to garage for tune-up, to install car safety restraints, to check spare tire and car emergency items.

☐ Have children examined by a doctor; get inoculations to avoid reactions on trip; get prescription refills, eyeglasses.

☐ Check all equipment before trip including camp gear, car gear, picnic gear and sports gear.

☐ Check and confirm all reservations.

**Packing Arrangements**

☐ Pack in small suitcases; label each with name and items.

☐ Have each child pack own toys/games with parental guidance (no small pieces with sharp edges).

☐ Have child keep security blanket/toy in car.

☐ Keep in car only what you expect to use while driving. (The rest belongs in car trunk or strapped onto car rack.)

**On the Road**

☐ Call ahead to reserve room(s) when necessary.

☐ Start out early in day or travel at night; limit distance traveled each day.

☐ Have children play/exercise just before getting into car.

☐ Stop car every two hours or so for comfort and outdoor play breaks. Keep lookout for safe swim areas, picnic grounds, fairs.

☐ Dress children for temperature inside car; take along sweater.

☐ Look for informal restaurants before hunger pangs strike. Avoid rush hours; take books, toys, crackers while sitting out waits in restaurants.

## Car Take-alongs

- pillow/blanket
- first-aid kit
- litter bags
- travel sick bag
- ___ motion sickness medication
- ___ plastic bags
- ___ damp washcloth in plastic/premoistened towelettes
- ___ tissues
- ___ chewing gum
- ___ mints
- _____
- _____
- _____

- non-messy snacks
  - ___ nuts
  - ___ raisins
  - ___ plain cookies
  - ___ crackers
  - ___ jar peanut butter/jelly
  - ___ cans of juice
  - ___ fruit
  - ___ hard candy

- picnic gear
  - ___ cooler/thermos
  - ___ paper cups/napkins
  - ___ plastic utensils
  - ___ powdered milk
  - ___ stock of simple breakfasts/lunches
  - ___ pure drinking water

- travel play bag
  - ___ pads/pencils
  - ___ coloring books
  - ___ markers/crayons
  - ___ puzzle fun books/pencil
  - ___ magic slate
  - ___ deck of cards
  - ___ small magnetic games
  - ___ pipe cleaners
  - ___ finger/hand puppets
  - ___ blunt scissors
  - ___ paperback books
  - ___ travel diary
  - ___ ball
  - ___ soft toy
  - ___ security blanket
- _____

## Car Safety

☐ Use seat belts and car safety restraints (suitable sizes) when car is in motion; do not start until everyone is "restrained." Do not let children use the same lap belt or share one with you.

☐ Have children sit in the back of the car; do not hold child on your lap in the front seat.

☐ Never leave sharp or heavy objects loose in car; keep rear window ledge clear.

☐ Never leave children alone in a car.

☐ Insist that children do not play with steering wheel, instrument panel, gearshift, door handles or locks.

☐ Forbid children to put their hands or head outside the window, to suck lollipop or popsicle stick while car is moving.

☐ Be strict about roughhousing and yelling in car.

# Vacation Packing List for Children

**Playwear**

☐ pants/slacks

___ dungarees

___ jogging

___ chino/corduroy

___ _____

___ _____

☐ sweaters/jackets

___ sweatshirt

___ Windbreaker

___ pullover

___ cardigan

___ sleeveless

___ _____

☐ shirts/blouses

___ polo shirts (long/short

sleeves)

___ _____

___ _____

☐ underwear

___ briefs

___ T-shirts

___ _____

___ _____

☐ sleepwear

___ pajamas/nightie

___ bathrobe

___ _____

☐ rain gear

___ slicker/hood

___ boots

☐ shoes

___ sneakers

___ sandals

___ hiking boots

___ _____

☐ socks

___ sweatsocks

___ high socks

___ _____

☐ cold weather

___ parka/vest

___ ski suit

___ winter jacket

___ snow boots

___ scarves/mittens/hats

___ thermal underwear

___ turtleneck tops

___ _____

☐ warm weather

___ bathing suit/trunks

___ bathing cap

___ beach shoes

___ beach robe

___ beach towel

___ shorts

___ baseball cap/straw hat

___ tank tops

___ _____

___ _____

**Dresswear**

☐ pants/slacks

___ _____

___ _____

___ _____

☐ shirts/blouses
___ white long-sleeved shirt
___ dressy/synthetic blouse
___ dress turtleneck

___ _____

___ _____

☐ suit
☐ jacket
___ blazer
___ velvet
___ tweed

___ _____

☐ dresses
___ short-sleeve print
___ knit
___ jumper/blouse

☐ skirts
___ cotton wrap-around
___ corduroy
___ pleated wool/synthetic

___ _____

___ _____

☐ accessories
___ ties
___ scarves
___ dress handkerchiefs
___ stockings/socks/tights
___ purse
___ jewelry

☐ shoes
___ dark leather
___ patent leather

___ _____

☐ outerwear

___ dress coat
___ all-weather coat/jacket
___ boots
___ gloves/hat/scarves

___ _____

___ _____

___ _____

**Sports Gear/Hobbies/Toys**

• stuffed animals

• cards

• jacks

• board games

• sketch pad/pencils/crayons

• books/magazines

• camera/film

• baseball mitt/softball

• tennis racket/balls

• Frisbee

• snorkel gear

• ski equipment

• _____

• _____

• _____

• _____

# First Aid Supply List for Camping

**Backpacker Minimum**

___ snakebite kit/fresh razor blade

___ water purification tablets

___ aspirin or substitute

___ antiseptic soap

___ cotton swabs

___ tweezers/needle/thread

___ scissors

___ moleskin

___ antibiotic ointment

___ burn ointment

___ assorted adhesive strip bandages

___ sterile gauze pads (4″×4″; 2″×2″)

___ gauze roll (2″)

___ adhesive tape roll (1″)

___ Ace bandage

___ safety pins

___ salt tablets

___ sunburn lotion

___ first-aid manual

___ medication alert

___ personal prescriptions

**For Car/Camping**

___ backpacker minimum

___ motion-sickness medication

___ poison-ivy medication

___ mild laxative

___ mild sedative

___ antacid

___ paper cups/measuring spoons

___ smelling salts

___ rubbing alcohol

___ cold packs

___ splints

___ triangular bandage

___ sheet/towels/blanket

___ _____

___ _____

# ✓ Checklist for Traveling with Pets

## Before Any Trip

☐ Make appointment with veterinarian:

    ___ get necessary shots

    ___ get current health and rabies vaccination certificates for state and international border checks

    ___ find out if flea collar is advised

    ___ ask what size pet container is right for your animal

    ___ check use of motion-sickness pills and/or tranquilizers; note frequency and timing on prescriptions

    ___ get diet instructions to carry out right before and during trip

    ___ find out what first-aid items pet might need

☐ Call or write in advance to find out if pet is welcome at place you will be staying.

☐ Plan to travel in early morning or late evening during warm weather.

☐ Give pet a chance to get used to portable kennel before actual confinement.

☐ Bathe, groom and exercise pet beforehand so animal can travel more comfortably.

## By Plane

☐ Call airline for latest regulations:

    ___ check age limitations (your pet may not be old enough to fly)

    ___ _____

☐ Book direct flight well in advance and try to avoid peak holiday periods.

☐ Make sure connecting flights can accommodate your pet; if possible, transfer pet yourself.

☐ Check if airline has approved crating container fitting the size of your pet. (One or two pets per flight are allowed to ride with passengers in under-the-seat containers.)

☐ Find out if other cargo in baggage compartment is harmful to your pet.

☐ Get to airport early and place animal in cage yourself; pick up immediately on arrival so container is not put on conveyor belt.

☐ If traveling to foreign country, get specific entry rules and forms from airline and/or consulate (a quarantine period may be required).

## Things to Remember en route in Car*

☐ Take pet for short rides in automobile before starting on trip so animal can get acclimated to motion of vehicle.

☐ Stop every few hours for exercise . . . park in shade . . . if you leave pet alone in car, keep windows slightly open, wider if pet is in a wire cage . . . never leash or tie up pet in car alone.

☐ Keep Thermos jug with crushed ice/water handy to wet towels and put on floor for pet to lie on (cats often get dizzy from fast-moving scenery).

☐ Dispose of unused canned food unless you have access to refrigerator . . . wait for main meal until end of day or when at destination.

☐ If you must leave pet alone in motel/hotel room, notify desk. Place the "Do Not Disturb" sign on door.

## Pet Container Checkup

● Is it large enough so pet can stand, turn, lie down?

● Is it strong, with nothing protruding inside?

● Is it made of nontoxic plastic with sturdy handle?

● Is the bottom leakproof?

● Does it offer cross-ventilation?

● Is it clearly marked with your name/address/telephone number, and marked LIVE ANIMAL with arrows showing upright position?

## Take-Along Items

● license tag

● I.D. collar

● health certificate

● rabies vaccination certificate

● leash/collar

● flea collar

● favorite toy

● dish

● food

● prescription/medication/tranquilizer

● Thermos jug

● towels

● pet container

● U. S. Customs Shippers Export Declaration

*Interstate travel with pets is not allowed on trains or buses with the exception of seeing-eye dogs; check local bus lines for their latest rules.

# ✔ Before-You-Go-on-Vacation List

- ☐ Arrange for care of pets, plants, lawn.

- ☐ Ask neighbor to collect your mail or have post office forward it.

- ☐ Pay important bills (mortgage/rent, car loans) due while you will be away.

- ☐ Stop home deliveries (newspapers) and notify of start-up date.

- ☐ Place important papers/valuables in safe-deposit box.

- ☐ Finalize vacation details:

  ___ check travel insurance coverage
  ___ get traveler's checks
  ___ refill prescriptions

  ___ repair/replace damaged luggage
  ___ check credit-card monetary limits
  ___ confirm reservations (plane/hotels/motels/car rentals)
  ___ have car checked
  ___ get road maps
  ___ _____

- ☐ Give neighbor key and have him/her check apartment/house and stock staples for your return.

- ☐ Leave itinerary with relative/friend.

- ☐ Notify police of period you will be away from home.

### Last-minute things to do

- Disconnect appliances.

- Check that kitchen equipment dials are turned to "off."

- Remove electric plugs from sockets.

- Turn down/off hot water/electricity.

- Set thermostat properly for heating/cooling while absent.

- Remove perishables from refrigerator/pantry.

- Close and lock windows/doors, including garage.

- Leave shades/blinds/drapes in usual position.

- Set burglar alarms/timers to turn on lights.

- Check that lights are off.

- Turn on phone-answering device.

- Take out garbage.

- _____

- _____

# At Work

☐ **Things to Remember When Asking for a Raise**

☐ **Checklist of Office Time-savers**

☐ **Things to Do When You Get Fired**

☐ **Things to Remember for a Job Interview**

☐ **List of Questions Interviewers Ask**

☐ **Employee Fringe Benefits Checklist**

☐ **New-Executive Checklist**

☐ **Checklist for Setting up a Business at Home**

☐ **Home-Based Small Business Idea List**

☐ **Retirement Checklist**

# ✓Things to Remember When Asking for a Raise

☐ Research your facts. See if you are at the top of the salary range for your job; find out the salary range of those jobs just below and above yours. Check out pay in competitive companies.

☐ Send your boss a memo before your annual salary review citing your accomplishments, where you may have fallen short, and ask if this accurately reflects your performance.

☐ Base the case for your raise on accomplishments, not your personal needs. Go in prepared to answer objections that may be made.

☐ Point out your specific contributions (in profits, efficiency, new ideas, problem solving) and their significance to the department and company goals.

☐ Document how your scope of work has enlarged, thus increasing your value; if you have taken on extra work in the area you want to move into, use this to indicate you are ready for a higher job classification.

☐ Specify the amount of your raise and ask for more than you are willing to settle for. But decide in advance if you will settle for: a title instead of a raise, a position with more responsibility but no pay increase; a new slot with a higher salary range with no immediate raise.

☐ Be prepared to negotiate a raise through expanded fringe benefits.

## When to Ask

☐ Be alert to the firm's financial picture. Know when the fiscal year starts. If possible, ask before the end of a good year and before a new budget is made.

☐ Make your request when your output is high or soon after you've been commended for some major work.

☐ Choose a day when your boss is "up" and when he's done some successful work for the company.

# ✓ Checklist of Office Time-savers

## Overall planning

☐ Write down your long-range goals.

☐ Keep a time log for several days to see how your time is spent; check if you are performing tasks each day that move your goals ahead.

☐ Tackle important tasks when your energy level is highest.

☐ Divide difficult jobs into manageable parts; learn to say "no" if that's what you mean.

☐ Set up deadlines and a daily schedule.

## Meetings

☐ Plan fewer meetings and start promptly.

☐ Go into every meeting with a clear idea of what you want to come out of it.

☐ Let everyone know in advance the purpose of the meeting and when it will end.

☐ Distribute an agenda and follow it. If meeting bogs down, adjourn to a definite time the next day.

☐ Make a faster exit; avoid holding conferences in your own office.

## Paperwork

☐ Keep desk surface clear except for work you intend to do that day.

☐ Have secretary sort your mail by category or by priority.

☐ Jot down a daily list of things to do; put items in order of priority; deal with them one at a time, working down your list.

☐ Try to not handle papers more than once; act on every piece you pick up; periodically review and discard old files.

☐ Never write a memo when a short note or quick call will do.

☐ Notify the appropriate people in writing if a project looks as if it will take longer than expected.

☐ Simplify reading and writing memos by creating a format others can follow.

☐ Develop form-type replies to be used in answering similar correspondence.

## Delegating

☐ Handle fewer details yourself; delegate work whenever possible; devise challenges to make routine work go faster.

☐ Train subordinates in specific areas so they can be of greater help to you.

☐ Let others pull together data you need to make a decision; set a deadline to keep people from spending too much time on one problem.

☐ Have your secretary take minutes of items requiring action during a meeting. Ask her/him to distribute them with due dates to those concerned and let her/him follow up.

## Interruptions

☐ Schedule at least an hour a day without interruptions.

☐ Set aside special times when you make and receive calls; specify certain days on a regular basis when you get to the office early or stay late to keep work from piling up.

☐ Keep your office door closed, but be available to people who need to confer.

☐ Try to deal with a person once a day and to handle all business with him/her at one time.

☐ Learn how to ease someone out of your office. (Try standing up or excusing yourself to make some important calls.)

☐ Use waiting or traveling time to mull over a problem, review a report, dictate a letter.

☐ Before you leave the office, know where you will begin the next day's work.

# Things to Do When You Get Fired

**Negotiate the Best Severance Deal You Can.**

Cover:

☐ Separation allowance
___ amount
___ what it covers
___ method of payment (increments may be preferable to lump sum)
___ duration (delayed payment may be to your advantage regarding taxes)

☐ Fringe benefits
___ life insurance
___ health insurance
___ accident policy
___ pension carryover provision
___ unused vacation pay
___ unused sick leave/personal days
___ profit sharing
___ stock options
___ car rental privileges
___ car allowance carryover
___ _____

☐ Office facilities
___ time to clear up loose ends
___ use of desk, telephone, copier
___ access to secretarial help
___ _____
___ _____

☐ Office handling
___ the terms of your contract, if applicable
___ announcement
___ incoming calls/mail
___ references
___ _____
___ _____

☐ Outplacement help
___ counseling (from inside company/by outside professionals)

___ leads
___ possible work by project/as consultant
___ _____
___ _____
___ _____

**Relieve Some of the Pressure You Are Under.**

Take these steps immediately:

☐ Tell your family the truth right away.

☐ Notify your creditors to see if you can postpone or refinance payments.

☐ File for unemployment benefits.

☐ Check grace period of health insurance extension. Arrange uninterrupted coverage (convert from office group or take out interim coverage).

☐ Look into Government benefits—you may be eligible for food stamps or other assistance.

☐ Find out job-hunting deductions allowed under IRS rules.

**Analyze Your Financial Picture for the Next Six Months.**

☐ Total usual monthly expenses
___ housing (rent/mortage)
___ household (utilities, heating, phone, etc.)
___ food
___ clothing/maintenance
___ transportation (public, car)
___ education
___ health
___ insurance payments
___ alimony

___ taxes

___ payments on debts

___ dues (membership/subscriptions/contributions)

___ personal (haircuts, gifts)

___ recreation

___ _____

___ _____

___ _____

☐ Figure ways to trim your life-style temporarily

___ budget cutbacks

___ alimony reduction

___ _____

___ _____

___ _____

___ _____

☐ Anticipate extra costs during this period

___ insurance premiums

___ equipment rental/secretarial

___ stationery/postage

___ telephone

___ transportation

___ research materials

___ _____

___ _____

___ _____

☐ List expected incoming money

___ severance pay

___ paycheck of other family member

___ unemployment check

___ savings bank interest

___ dividends

___ other income/interest from investments

___ repayment of debts

___ tax refund

___ _____

___ _____

___ _____

☐ Figure out how to generate extra cash if necessary

___ assets which can be converted

___ _____

___ _____

___ loans

___ part-time/temporary job

___ _____

___ _____

## Figure Out What You Want to Do Next.

☐ List aspects of the job you liked best and least

☐ List your strengths, your weak areas

☐ This is the time to:

___ find a similar job

___ stay in same field but do different work

___ change your career

___ start your own business

___ _____

___ _____

## Tackle Your Job Hunt Strategy as if It Were a New Job.

☐ Prepare an updated résumé

☐ Make master list of contacts (names, titles, addresses, phone numbers)

___ business peers

___ people working for the competition

___ friends

___ people you knew in school

___ individuals in key spots in companies that interest you

___ _____

___ _____

___ _____

☐ Research
    ___ newly promoted people
    ___ upcoming job openings
    ___ companies you plan to contact
    ___ latest developments in field
    ___ conferences to attend
    ___ study trade journals/newspapers

☐ Develop cover letters
    ___ for companies you would like to work for
    ___ for search firms
    ___ _____
    ___ _____

☐ Register with employment agencies specializing in your field

☐ Join job-hunting clubs (40-Plus, Sales Executive Club, etc.)

☐ Anticipate questions interviewers ask
    ___ tape/videotape practice interviews

☐ Plan your daily "follow-up" schedule the day before
    ___ answer ads
    ___ make telephone calls

___ set up interviews
___ correspondence
___ develop new leads
___ maintain recordkeeping
    • job-hunting expenses
    • update contact list
    • file on information sources
    • ads answered
    • companies résumé sent to/responses

**Evaluate Why You Were Fired so You Are Not Caught Unprepared in an Interview or on Your Next Job.**

☐ merger consolidation
☐ reorganization
☐ economy layoff
☐ forced resignation/early retirement
☐ political infighting
☐ personality clash
☐ incompetence/non-performance
☐ promoted beyond ability/readiness
☐ insubordination/indiscretion
☐ _____
☐ _____

## *Résumé Checkup*

- neat, well-printed copies

- no misspellings or erasures

- one standard-size page, preferably

- include name/home address/telephone number

- omit age/sex/race/religion/marital status

- concise work history with last job first

- use problem/action/result format to describe responsibilities

- education/special training/associations to which you belong

- indicate references on request

- state salary requirements are competitive

# ✓ Things to Remember for a Job Interview

**Before**

☐ Learn all you can about potential employer.

    ____ Read the annual report, if possible.
    ____ Note where firm stands with the competition.
    ____ Figure out what its major problems may be.

☐ Find out what qualifications the company seeks.

    ____ Understand the functions of the specific job.
    ____ Know the going rate for similar positions.

☐ Prepare anecdotes to illustrate your strong points.

    ____ problem solving
    ____ dealing with people
    ____ _____    ____ _____
    ____ _____    ____ _____
    ____ _____    ____ _____

☐ Think through questions you are likely to be asked.

☐ Dress so you feel comfortable and look confident.

☐ Plan to arrive early and check your appearance.

**During**

☐ Never knock present or former employer.

☐ Avoid simple Yes or No answers, unless explicitly called for.

☐ Disguise your weak points by underscoring the positive side.

☐ Explain how your experience/skills make you the right person for this job/company.

    ____ Detail how you contributed to increased efficiency/profits.
    ____ Use terms that show you know the field.
    ____ Ask questions that reveal you studied up on the company.
    ____ Demonstrate your interest by making practical suggestions.

☐ Discuss salary range after you have sold your qualifications.

    ___ Ask for more than you are willing to settle for.
    ___ Try to negotiate fringe benefits.
    ___ Treat benefits as part of your salary package if asked to state current compensation.

☐ Glean what the negative aspects of the job/organization might be.

☐ Ask questions that will help you determine if this is the right job:

    ___ What are the possibilities for growth/advancement?
    ___ Why (and where) did person who held job go?
    ___ How many people would have to okay decisions made by you?
    ___ What is the official job classification?
    ___ What is the policy on salary review?
    ___ What are the fringe benefits?
    ___ Who would you report to and what is this person's position?

    ___ _____

    ___ _____

☐ Leave extra copies of your résumé with interviewer.

## After

☐ Send a follow-up letter.

    ___ Restate what went well.
    ___ Correct what did not go well, if possible.

☐ Telephone to see if any decision has been made. (Wait a week.)

# ✓List of Questions Interviewers Ask

Are you prepared to answer them?

## About Your Past/Present Experience

☐ Why did you leave your last job?

☐ Why do you want to leave your present job?

☐ Were you fired from your last job? Why?

☐ What do/did you like/dislike about your job?

☐ How would you evaluate your present firm?

☐ What do you think of your boss?

☐ How do you think people who work under you would describe you?

☐ What problems have you identified/solved in your present job that had been overlooked?

☐ Name some instances where your work has been criticized.

☐ What are your biggest accomplishments, workwise? Your worst failures?

☐ Why did you choose this field?

☐ Which of your jobs did you like best . . . least . . . why?

☐ How do you explain the gaps between jobs?

☐ What was your previous salary . . . current salary?

## About Your Prospective Job

☐ Why do you want this job or want to work for this company?

☐ What interests you most and least about this position?

☐ What makes you think you can do the job?

☐ Are you available to travel/work overtime?

☐ How long would it take you to make a contribution to this firm?

☐ How do we know you won't leave in a year . . . how long would you stay?

☐ What other jobs are you considering?

## Personal

☐ What are your strengths . . . shortcomings?

☐ How would you describe your personality?

☐ How do you work under pressure?

☐ What kind of person would you like to work for?

☐ What kind of boss would you be?

☐ Do you prefer staff or line work?

☐ How do you get along with people?

☐ How is your financial situation?

☐ Why aren't you earning more at your age?

☐ How much do you expect to be earning in ten years?

☐ What do you plan to be doing five to ten years from now?

☐ If you could start again, what would you do differently?

☐ What would your ideal job be?

# ✓ Employee Fringe Benefits Checklist

The type and amount of benefits provided by employers vary widely. When comparing them, check:

___ benefit eligibility requirements
___ duration/extent of each benefit
___ what employer contributes
___ what you contribute
___ policy on leaving or job termination
___ what percent of salary fringe benefits represent

## Insurance

☐ major medical plan
☐ dental/eye care plan
☐ disability plan
☐ group life/accidental death
☐ travel accident benefits
☐ conversion privileges from group to individual policies
☐ group insurance rates for homeowner's/car policies

## Profit Sharing

☐ cash bonus plan
☐ stock bonus
☐ employee stock purchase plan
☐ wage and salary dividend
☐ employee savings plan (vesting mechanism)

## Recreational

☐ travel discounts
☐ car-rental discounts
☐ paid memberships in health/athletic/country clubs
☐ use of company resort (free/low cost)
☐ employee recreational facility/social/athletics program

## Time

☐ overtime pay/compensatory time off
☐ flextime
☐ four-day work week
☐ maternity/paternity leave
☐ paid time off
   ___ sick days/medical illness/disability
   ___ vacations
   ___ holidays
   ___ religious observances
   ___ bereavement pay
   ___ jury duty
   ___ personal days
☐ time off without pay
   ___ educational leave of absence
☐ periodic performance review/merit increases
☐ annual renegotiation of contract/cost-of-living increases
☐ severance period

## Retirement

- ☐ early retirement option
- ☐ annuity/pension plans (vesting mechanism)
- ☐ retirement trust fund (deferred payment option)
- ☐ continuing insurance benefits

## Services (free/low-cost)

- ☐ paid membership in professional/trade associations
- ☐ personal legal / accounting / financial / planning
- ☐ thrift or savings plan / credit union / emergency loans
- ☐ outplacement/retirement counseling
- ☐ day care for preschoolers

- ☐ adoption expenses aid
- ☐ relocation service/expenses/allowance
- ☐ rent-free housing
- ☐ free parking
- ☐ travel expenses
- ☐ meals in company cafeteria
- ☐ medical dispensary/annual physical exam
- ☐ discounts on company products/services
- ☐ paid funerals for employees

## Educational

- ☐ tuition aid/reimbursement program
- ☐ college scholarship program for children of employees
- ☐ advanced education employee fellowship
- ☐ specialized on-the-job training

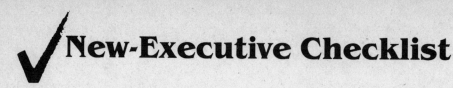
# New-Executive Checklist

## Learn the Job Before You Suggest Any Major Changes

- Answer calls and letters personally at the beginning to spot bottlenecks in the daily operation; set up a chart to increase efficiency.

- Resist transferring or terminating secretary, office workers; find out what they know about office politics and/or problems that you may have inherited.

- Read through the files left by your predecessor.

- Examine job descriptions of those who report to you; make sure they are current.

- Find out what your expense account covers from the person who approves it; ask how often to submit it and how detailed it should be.

- Listen carefully to peers to glean important information during your early days on the job.

- Join associations of people in like positions to learn more about competitive practices and applicable ideas for your company.

## Establish Yourself with the Staff

- Sit down with office manager in charge of new offices to expedite getting yours finished.

- Find out who does what efficiently. If possible, contact the person who held your position to ask about working habits of your superiors and subordinates.

- Make subordinates feel comfortable without getting overly friendly. Encourage them to talk about their ambitions and gradually build up their loyalty.

- Keep scheduled appointments with your staff.

- Be specific in your instructions and deadlines to minimize communications mishaps.

- Promote free exchange of ideas at brainstorming sessions. Invite quantity of input and wild notions without fear of putdowns or evaluations.

- Allow subordinates to make noncrucial decisions and mistakes. (It helps train them and points up your skill as a supervisor.)

- Hand out as many compliments as criticisms; give credit when due.

- Keep your personal life out of the office; avoid cliques and discourage gossip.

- Censure behind closed doors early in the day. Later, reassure the person you are confident things will work out better.

- Use "List of Questions Interviewers Ask" if you are hiring people for the first time.

## Establish Yourself with the Boss

- Clarify the lines of authority if necessary. Find out what areas of decision-making are your responsibility and what areas must be discussed beforehand.

- Submit status reports on your projects on a monthly basis.

- Answer memos that call for action promptly. If you disagree, put yourself on record without feeling that your job is on the line. (A contrary opinion backed up with reasons may not get the boss's okay, but it is likely to gain his/her respect.)

- As you feel more confident, start taking risks that give you a chance for innovative successes.

# ✓ Checklist for Setting Up a Business at Home

☐ Do you have the self-discipline required to run a business from your home? How will it affect your family activities?

☐ Does the product you make or sell, or the service you want to perform, fill a need in your community? In what ways can you improve on the competition?

☐ Do you know how to make, or where to get the product you want to sell? Do you know what you need to supply the service?

☐ Have you estimated operating costs for the first year? How much money do you need to start?

☐ How much of your own money can you put into the business? Where can you borrow additional capital?

☐ Have you checked the legalities for a home-based business?

- zoning regulations/restrictions
- licenses/permits/taxes/insurance
- special laws for your line of business
- registration of business name/business structure/liability

☐ What record-keeping systems and forms will work best for you? What financial statements will you need? Do you know the current federal tax requirements for business use of a home? Have you an accountant?

☐ Have you worked out operational procedures? What prices will you need to charge to make a profit? How do these compare with your competitors?

☐ Do you know who your potential customers are? What are their characteristics, by age, sex, income level, address? Have you contacted accredited trade/business associations in your area?

☐ Does your location present any problem?

- neighborhood
- parking space
- access by public transportation

☐ What are your minimal work-space requirements?

- private area (separate from living quarters)
- separate entrance
- reception-selling area

- office record-keeping area
- workroom-storage area

____ square footage
____ ventilation/acoustics
____ lighting/outlets/voltage
____ _____

- outbuildings/land

☐ Will you be able to hire outside help if needed? What special services will you require?

- clerical
- maintenance/cleaning
- selling/craft workers
- pickup and delivery
- advertising/publicity
- _____

☐ What are your minimal equipment-supply requirements?

- reception-selling area

____ seating
____ display units
____ wall decor
____ _____

____ _____

- office record-keeping area

____ intercom
____ desk/chair/lighting
____ typewriter/table
____ file cabinets/business forms/postage scale
____ copier/calculator/adding machine/cash register
____ telephone/phone-answering machine
____ desk accessories/office supplies

- workroom-storage area

____ large tables/seating
____ work surfaces/storage units/shelving
____ security devices
____ specialized equipment
____ _____

____ _____

____ _____

# ✔ Home-Based Small Business Idea List

### Services

- ____ employment agency
- ____ baby-sitting registry
- ____ real-estate agency
- ____ roommate search
- ____ barter-swap bureau
- ____ collector's exchange
- ____ membership club
  - • discount entertainment
  - • single parents
  - • _____
- ____ travel agency
- ____ bed and breakfast stopovers
- ____ sightseeing service
- ____ chauffeuring/taxi service
- ____ party planning
- ____ catering
- ____ shopping/errand service
- ____ medical accessory rental
- ____ child day care
- ____ pet grooming
- ____ haircutting
- ____ lending library
- ____ bookbinding center
- ____ plastic laminating
- ____ frame-making
- ____ portrait photography
- ____ dressmaking/alterations
- ____ interior decorating
- ____ wallpaper/painting
- ____ closet and cabinet organizing
- ____ carpentry
- ____ power tool rentals
- ____ tool sharpening service
- ____ furniture stripping/restoration
- ____ small appliance repairs
- ____ plumbing
- ____ electrical contractor/repairs
- ____ bookkeeping
- ____ dictaphone/typing service

### Services

- ____ telephone-answering
- ____ telephone market research
- ____ cataloging service
- ____ window display service
- ____ tape record local speeches
- ____ film/projector rentals
- ____ publish local shoppers
- ____ compile directories/guides
- ____ information research
- ____ clipping service
- ____ public relations
- ____ copy editing/proofreading
- ____ writing
- ____ translating
- ____ literary agency
- ____ mail order
  - • hobby kits
  - • stationery supplies
  - • astrology
  - • building plans
  - • financial advice
  - • _____
  - • _____
- ____ sales representative
  - • cosmetics
  - • household goods
  - • magazine subscriptions
  - • _____
  - • _____
- ____ home lessons/tutoring
  - • cooking
  - • languages
  - • music
  - • knitting
  - • handcrafts
  - • _____
  - • _____
- ____ collection agency
- ____ _____
- ____ _____
- ____ _____
- ____ _____

### Goods

- ____ hobby outlet
- ____ art gallery
- ____ antiques
- ____ books
- ____ handcrafts
  - • ceramics
  - • candles
  - • custom-woven rugs
  - • needlepoint
  - • batik T-shirts
  - • miniatures
  - • toys
  - • jewelry
  - • knitted/crotcheted items
  - • _____
- ____ homemade items
  - • candy
  - • baked goods
  - • preserves/relishes
  - • scented soaps/sachets
  - • _____
  - • _____
- ____ garden products
  - • plants
  - • produce
  - • herbs
  - • _____
- ____ paper flower decorations
  - • _____
  - • _____
- ____ stamps/coins
- ____ nostalgia/comics
- ____ secondhand/surplus sales
- ____ used furniture
- ____ special clothes
- ____ beauty boutique
- ____ discount fabrics
- ____ _____
- ____ _____
- ____ _____

# ✓ Retirement Checklist

☐ Have you checked your earnings record with the social security headquarters in Baltimore, Maryland (21235) within the last three years? Request:

    ___ a statement of your payment record
    ___ an estimate of your monthly benefit amount
    ___ an estimate of benefits covering other family members

☐ Have your considered your retirement options under social security? Do you know what you would be entitled to if you:

    ___ retire at age 62 on a reduced benefit
    ___ retire at age 65 on a full benefit
    ___ work past 65 and get a bonus for each year you defer your benefits
    ___ continue to work until age 70 (or later) and receive full benefits regardless of how much money you earn

☐ If not covered by a company pension, or if self-employed, have you set up your own retirement plan? Have you checked:

    ___ different types of IRA/Keogh plans/different investment vehicles
    ___ a particular plan with your lawyer/accountant to make sure it suits your retirement needs

☐ If your company/union has a pension plan, are you clear about its eligibility requirements? How its provisions can affect your benefits? Ask for a copy of the Summary Plan Description. Note:

    ___ how old you must be to qualify/how long with the company
    ___ if your social security benefits are deducted from your pension
    ___ if your benefits will be reduced by early retirement or a joint and survivor's option
    ___ if cost-of-living increases are included
    ___ what the pay-out options are

☐ Have you asked your employer for a personal accounting of your pension credits to date? Do you know:

    ___ how much your employer contributes

    ___ how much you contribute (what percent of your compensation)
    ___ when your benefits become non-forfeitable (vested)
    ___ if the plan is insured by the Pension Benefit Guaranty Corporation

☐ Do you know what happens to your health insurance coverage when you reach age 65? Ask your employer:

    ___ if your group medical and disability coverage continues
    ___ if the company pays any part of the premiums after retirement/if you can buy additional coverage
    ___ if you can convert group to an individual policy when you leave the job

Ask your insurance agent:
    ___ if you will still be protected in case of extended illness/convalescent care/disability
    ___ if your policy(ies) are guaranteed renewable
    ___ how you can supplement medicare benefits (look into health maintenance organizations)

Ask local social security office (three months before you are 65):
    ___ about applying for medicare hospital coverage
    ___ about applying for medicare medical coverage

☐ Have you reviewed all your potential sources of retirement income? (Check with your IRS/accountant to see how funds from different sources affect your tax situation.)

    ___ savings
    ___ social security/veteran's benefits
    ___ pension/personal retirement account
    ___ profit-sharing plan
    ___ life insurance/annuities
    ___ dividends from securities
    ___ business investments
    ___ gifts/bequests/inheritance
    ___ part-time job
    ___ _____
    ___ _____

# Where You Live

☐ **Things to Consider Before Buying a Condo/Co-op**

☐ **Apartment Renter's Checklist**

☐ **House Hunter's Checklist**

☐ **House Buyer's Checklist**

☐ **Things to Do Before the Closing**

☐ **House Seller's Checklist**

☐ **Things to Do Before You Rent Out/ Sublet/Swap Your Home**

# Things to Consider Before Buying a Condo/Co-op*

How Ownership in a Condominium and a Cooperative Differ

### If You Buy a Condo

- you own your individual unit

- you receive a deed to it

- you jointly own the common areas; this is an "undivided interest" in common areas and facilities (streets, land under building, pool, courts, heating plant, hallways, etc.) that you share with your co-owners

- you may obtain a mortage to finance your purchase

- you pay mortgage payments and real-estate taxes directly to bank and/or local government

- your monthly carrying charges are based on your percentage share of the costs of maintaining, operating, insuring the common areas

- you are not liable if other unit owners do not pay their real-estate taxes or mortgage obligations

- you get the same tax benefits as a homeowner

- your votes in the condo association represent your "undivided interest percentage" (the proportionate value of your unit to the total of all units)

- you may lease or sell your unit independent of other owners

- you and the other owners elect a board of governors who govern the common estate

### If You Buy a Co-op

- you do not directly own your individual unit; you own stock in the corporation that owns the multi-unit property

- the corporation, not you, holds title to your building

- you receive a long-term proprietary lease

- if you don't have the cash to buy the stock, you can use the stock and lease as security for a co-op loan; your loan payments will be in addition to your monthly maintenance fee

- the corporation directly assumes the obligations to finance and operate the property

*Statutes on multi-unit property ownership differ from state to state; the fine points may vary even from project to project in states without strong regulations. This checklist will help you find out what you need to know; it is not a substitute for the professional help you should have before you buy.

- your monthly carrying charges are your proportionate share of all costs including mortgage, insurance and real-estate taxes

- you can be assessed when other stockholders fail to pay their share of the monthly mortgage and maintenance charges

- you are entitled to deduct a proportionate share of the taxes and mortgage interest paid by the corporation from your personal income tax

- the price you pay for your unit as well as your monthly maintenance fee depend on the number of shares of stock allocated to your unit

- you need written permission of the board of directors of the co-op corporation to sublease and to sell your stock and transfer your lease

- you and the other stockholders elect a board of directors which makes decisions on operating the co-op corporation

☐ Be sure you receive and read copies of all the basic documents for condo/co-op you are considering:

Co-op
___ prospectus (look for tax opinion)
___ proprietary lease
___ bylaws
___ operating budget
___ management agreement
___ subscription agreement
___ mortgage (maturity date, etc.)
___ building/zoning plans in area
___ ground lease (if any)

Condo
___ prospectus
___ declaration of covenants, conditions and restrictions (also known as master deed)
___ bylaws
___ operating budget
___ management agreement
___ regulatory agreement (if mortgage is HUD/FHA-insured)
___ survey and plan
___ purchase agreement or sales contract
___ recreation lease (if any)

☐ For a condo/co-op resale, also ask to see:

___ the most recent assessed value statement

___ notarized evidence of any unpaid assessments, taxes, etc. owed on unit offered for sale

___ current financial statement (of condo association/co-op corporation), including scheduled capital expenditures and amount of reserves

___ copies of casualty and liability policies

___ title/judgment and lien search

☐ If project is incomplete or new:

___ check with state regulatory agency

___ find out if developer has plans to enlarge the project at a later date

___ get a written timetable for completion and guarantee of deposit refund

___ know what the extras are in the model unit

___ ask if furnishings are included

___ find out how many units are unsold/ how many are rented out by developer/ sponsor

☐ If building is being converted from a rental, find out:

___ the reputation of the seller/sponsor

___ how large a percentage of tenants chose to buy in

___ how the budget of the rental compares with the estimated maintenance under the new ownership form

___ what the engineering report reveals about building's condition

___ what major renovations/repairs still need to be done

___ if there are sufficient funds in the reserve fund to cover prior neglect/contingencies

___ if the governors/directors want to improve the project by increasing maintenance costs or if they are trying to keep the established maintenance

☐ Decide if the house rules (in condo declaration/in co-op proprietary lease) will hinder your enjoyment and/or use of the property. Check restrictions on:

___ children/their use of recreational areas

___ pets

___ use of facilities by guests

___ outdoor cooking

___ hours of use for facilities (laundry/pool, etc.)

___ renting out

___ noise

___ landscaping/gardening

___ storage

___ garage

## Questions to Ask

Keep them in mind as you read over the basic documents.

☐ Are house rules and restrictions on use of the property the same for all?

☐ What are the itemized monthly expenses? Will you have to pay extra for:

___ utilities

___ parking space

___ recreational facilities/TV cable

☐ What is the individual condo owner/co-op stockholder responsible for as far as exterior and interior repairs and upkeep? What is the responsibility of the governing board?

☐ How much control over the condo/co-op does the developer/sponsor retain? For how long?

☐ Is the developer/sponsor also the managing agent? Is the managing agent under the supervision of the Board?

☐ On what basis are ownership, assessments and voting rights figured?

☐ What constitutes a majority and a quorum for doing business?

☐ Does any decision or change require a 100 percent vote?

☐ What percentage of votes is needed to:

___ approve the annual budget
___ amend the bylaws
___ change the governing board
___ remove the manager

☐ What control does the Board have over resale? Right of first refusal? Approval of prospective buyers?

## Especially for Condo Buyers

☐ What are boundaries of the common areas and of your property as a unit owner?

☐ Are common areas owned by the condo association or the developer and only leased? If so, who is responsible for maintenance?

☐ Is the condo association or city responsible for repairing the streets?

## Especially for Co-op Buyers

☐ Is the lease inseparable from the stock? Are all stockholders occupants?

☐ What are the terms of subleasing?

☐ Is voting decided by number of shares held or by one vote per stockholder?

☐ On what basis were shares in the corporation allocated to each apartment? How can they be reallocated or additional ones issued?

☐ What percentage of your maintenance is tax-deductible?

### *Before Your Sign Any Sales Contract or Subscription Agreement*

• Ask a lawyer familiar with condo/co-op regulations in your state to go over all the basic documents.

• Have a banker look over the mortgage financing of the building to see if large assessments are likely in the near future.

• Have your accountant check out possible tax benefits.

# ✓ Apartment Renter's Checklist

☐ Have you checked out the neighborhood? Is it safe, convenient to public transportation? How are the neighborhood schools?

☐ Have you leads on apartments in desired areas from doormen, friends, storekeepers, classified ads, local bulletin boards, rental agents?

☐ Do you know the going rental rates for high risers, town houses, older and new apartments?

☐ What is most important to you and what are you willing to forgo in an apartment rental?

    ____ elevator(s)
    ____ high floor/view
    ____ terrace
    ____ doorman service
    ____ porter(s)/maintenance staff
    ____ service entrance
    ____ basement storage/bicycle/carriage room
    ____ laundry facilities: in basement/on floor/in apartment
    ____ garage: indoor/outdoor
    ____ recreational facilities/playground area
    ____ private entrance/backyard
    ____ bright sunny exposure/cross-ventilation
    ____ space requirements
    ____ efficient kitchen/equipment
    ____ modern bathrooms
    ____ air conditioning
    ____ closet space

☐ Is the apartment building you are considering a safe one? Have you talked to other tenants in the building? (Ask about any special problems.) Do they have:

    ____ 24-hour doorman or locked entrances
    ____ intercom system
    ____ closed-circuit TV in lobby
    ____ compliance with fire-code standards (fire stairwells, etc.)
    ____ well lighted hallways/outside entrance
    ____ laundry room with specified hours of use
    ____ no public parking facility in basement (unless locked entry to rest of building)

☐ Is your tenancy protected by any form of rent control?

    ____ check state/local laws

☐ Have you checked the lease? Does the lease spell out what you and the landlord agreed to verbally? Understand all the terms and conditions before you sign:

    ____ amount of rent/due date/late-payment penalty
    ____ who pays for utilities/exterminator/car space/repairs
    ____ amount of security deposit
    ____ sublet clause
    ____ rent escalator clause
    ____ length of lease/renewal rent increase
    ____ termination/renewal conditions
    ____ advance notice from landlord to inspect premises
    ____ living conditions (children/noise/pets/business use)
    ____ emergency repairs/complaints procedure

☐ What happens if building is converted to a co-op/condo? Does the lease cover this contingency?

### Before You Sign

- Submit a list of existing conditions that need repair to landlord; retain a copy.

- Find out address/telephone number of authorized person to handle problems that may arise.

# ✓ House Hunter's Checklist

☐ Investigate where you and your family want to live. Observe and compare neighborhoods; check local real-estate ads; speak to merchants, residents and real-estate agents. Ask:

___ How convenient is area to your job?

___ Is public transportation easily available?

___ Are the schools in the district of good quality? Near enough?

___ Is shopping convenient?

___ Are cultural/recreational facilities/religious centers within reasonable distance?

___ What is the community mix? (ages, backgrounds)

___ How built up is the area? Does it seem to be undergoing major changes?

___ Are roads/streets well maintained?

___ Are neighborhood houses in good condition?

___ Are there noticeable nuisances? (neighborhood noise, odors)

___ Is there heavy commuter/truck traffic nearby?

___ Are there health hazards close by? (toxic fumes, landfills)

___ Is community water supply sufficient, safe? Sewage disposal system adequate?

___ Is fire/police protection efficient? What are area crime problems?

___ Is there a good medical facility/hospital in area?

☐ Get facts and figures from local government/tax/school offices. Find out:

___ current zoning regulations . . . surrounding areas . . . future plans . . . if variances are granted easily

___ plans to develop industry . . . roads

___ property tax rates . . . how they are assessed . . . if increasing . . . at what rate

___ if new schools are planned . . . how they will be financed . . . the expenditure per pupil

___ if school board is elected from the local community

___ what recreational/educational/safety/sanitation services are included in the community budget

☐ Review your overall housing preferences and needs including type and style of home. Consider if family size is likely to increase or decrease in the next five years or so. Think about:

___ the space in square footage required by your family . . . how many bedrooms are adequate

___ special needs of family members that require a special location/rooms/architectural features

___ easy maintenance as a priority . . . do-it-yourself repairs and upkeep

___ how important privacy/outdoor space is to you . . . the minimum amount of property you want

☐ Figure the amount of money you can spend on the purchase price of home. (Rule of thumb: about two and one half times annual family income.) Estimate initial and ongoing house-related costs.

## Cash needed immediately

___ down payment

___ closing costs

___ professional fees (lawyer/engineer/house appraiser)

___ moving costs

___ appliances/furnishings

___ emergency reserve fund

## Monthly housing costs

___ mortgage payments (principal and interest)

___ taxes for property/school/special assessments

___ maintenance/repair service

___ fuel

___ utilities (gas/electric/water/telephone)

___ property insurance

☐ Keep accurate records as you compare monthly housing costs in specific communities. Note asking prices, what is included, special features of houses that seem acceptable to you.

# ✓ House Buyer's Checklist

☐ Zero in on two or three homes that are acceptable to you and your family. Check out the one you like best.

☐ Consider if you need an engineer or other professional to check out the basic soundness of the house.

___ Can you tell if the roof is leakproof?

___ Are the outside chimneys in good repair?

___ Is the foundation cracked? Well above ground?

___ Is the basement dry?

___ Can you tell if there are termites? Wood rot?

___ Is the attic dry? Well insulated? Vented?

___ Is the home well insulated?

___ Can you tell if there is adequate electric supply into the home?

___ Is the plumbing system in good repair? Pressure adequate?

___ Is plumbing connected to city sewers?

___ What is the source of water supply?

___ Can you tell if the heating/cooling system is efficient? What type is it?

___ Is hot-water supply adequate?

___ Does land slope away from house foundation? Is it landscaped to prevent erosion?

___ Do inside rooms have damp plaster walls?

___ Are floors in good repair? Do they sag? Tilt?

☐ See if the house fills the living needs of you and your family now and in the future:

___ convenient layout

___ separate bedroom wing/upstairs bedrooms

___ enough bathrooms

___ den/family playroom

___ good daytime light

___ separate entry doors for different parts of the house

___ access to rooms without crossing through other rooms

___ convenient garage location/large enough

___ well-planned kitchen: enough cupboards/countertops/outlets/ventilation

___ enough closets

___ storage space for lawn/maintenance equipment

___ ample privacy around home/pleasant view

___ possibilities for enlargement

☐ Revisit the house several times. Make sure that you have inspected everything thoroughly, the owners have answered all your questions and have produced necessary records. Ask for:

___ fuel bills for the last two years

___ tax bills for property/school

___ legal records of liens/easements

___ the latest assessment on the house/next reassessment date

____ utility bills for the last two years: electric/gas/water

____ survey map of property

☐ Find out how long house has been on the market, what you will have to spend for repairs and improvement; make your first offer less than the asking price. Find out what the owner plans to leave and what is negotiable.

____ carpeting

____ lighting fixtures/chandeliers

____ draperies/blinds/shades

____ refrigerator/stove

____ portable dishwasher

____ washer/dryer

____ lawn maintenance equipment

____ bookshelves/furniture

____ TV antenna/rotor

____ storms/screens

☐ When buying a new home from a model in a development, check with sellers/developers. Find out what is/is not included on your site and in your home. (Speak with previous buyers of the builder's house if you can.)

____ Look at your lot carefully for size/drainage/view.

____ Find out who pays for roads/sidewalks/sewer connections/utility wires/water connection, or if well must be drilled.

____ Get a completion date in writing/penalty clause.

____ Find out what extras are shown in model and not included in the house.

____ Check what warranties/guarantees cover.

____ Find out how your land will be graded/landscaped.

☐ Get your own lawyer to represent you before you sign any papers or leave a deposit; understand all the terms of the purchase contract. Ask:

____ Under what circumstances can you/owner cancel without penalty?

____ Who will hold down payment in escrow? Will it earn interest? Who gets it?

____ How will you finance the specified purchase price of the house?

____ Who pays for the various costs at the closing?

____ Have you arranged a title search . . . insurance?

____ Must the home pass professional inspection?

____ Is there a fixed date when you get possession of the home . . . items included in sale?

☐ Shop around for the best mortgage terms by investigating various loan sources and programs. Compare:

____ interest rate (and points at closing)

____ time period of repayment

____ prepayment penalty . . . assumption of mortgage by future buyer

____ future advances clause

____ grace period . . . late payment charges

____ closing cost charged by lender

# ✔ Things to Do Before the Closing

☐ Do you have your own lawyer to represent your interests? What do lawyer's fees cover?

☐ Have you taken care of problems relating to liens, judgments or easements on the property, riparian rights, restrictive covenants?

☐ Have you checked that your mortgage is firmly secured?

☐ Have all the needed documents from local/state authorities been supplied?

___ certificate of occupancy
___ plumbing/sewer installation certificates
___ code compliance certificates (wiring, etc.)
___ zoning variance
___ _____
___ _____

☐ Do you know which of the following closing costs are applicable in your case? (Settlement services and charges vary from area to area; get a good-faith estimate from lender; you can obtain a list of actual costs one business day before the closing.)

___ Related to loan

- loan origination fee (a percentage of the loan)
- loan discount (often called "points")
- appraisal fee
- credit report
- lender's inspection fee
- mortgage insurance application fee
- assumption fee
- _____
- _____

___ Advance payments required by lender

- interest
- mortgage insurance premium
- hazard insurance premium
- _____
- _____

___ Reserves deposited with lender ("escrow" accounts)

- hazard insurance (may be included in homeowner's policy)
- mortgage insurance
- city property taxes
- county property taxes
- annual assessments
- _____
- _____

___ Related to title

- closing fee
- title search
- title examination
- title insurance binder
- document preparation
- notary fees
- lawyer's fees
- title insurance (lender's and owner's)
- survey
- _____
- _____

\_\_\_ Miscellaneous additional charges
- government recording fees (deed and mortgage)
- city/county tax/stamps
- state tax/stamps
- pest inspection
- _____
- _____

☐ Does lender require title insurance and survey? Do you want to purchase an owner's title insurance policy as well?

☐ Have you asked lender for a copy of the appraisal report?

☐ Have you purchased homeowner's insurance?

☐ Have you arranged to inspect the house right before you take title to make sure everything is in working order?

☐ Have you enough funds in checking account to cover all your "closing" checks?

☐ Does your down-payment check have to be certified? Are the proceeds held in escrow until closing?

### Closing-Day Reminders

- Bring your copy of purchase contract; have your lawyer check that terms have been met.

- Bring copy of homeowner's policy (or paid receipt) if required by lender.

- Check that you have all warranties/guarantees/certification documents connected with home.

- Be prepared to finalize adjustments with seller for prepaid items such as fuel oil, prepaid insurance and taxes.

- Understand all papers before signing; get copies for your records.

- Get receipts for all payments.

- Arrange to register transfer of deed.

- Get house key(s).

- Arrange for utility connections.

# ✔ House Seller's Checklist

☐ Examine your house (starting from the outside) as if you were the prospective buyer. Note what needs fixing; figure that the more visible the improvement, the more salable its value. Before showing home:
    ___ spruce up kitchen/bathrooms (most salable rooms)
    ___ fix leaky/noisy plumbing
    ___ paint peeling/dirty walls
    ___ repair broken steps
    ___ spruce up landscaping (mow lawn, etc.)
    ___ get rid of clutter in closets/basement/attic
    ___ clean house thoroughly (straighten before each showing)

☐ Decide if you want to sell home yourself, list with real-estate broker(s) for a percentage of the selling price or a flat-fee service. (Stay in background when agent shows your home.)

☐ If you decide to sign up with a realtor, clarify:

    ___ listing service offered
    ___ type of fee/when payable
    ___ realtor not entitled to any commission unless house is brought through closing
    ___ period of time agent has to sell your house
    ___ terms for renewal/cessation
    ___ what agent will do for you
      • advertise
      • show home
      • negotiate
      • evaluate if potential buyer is qualified
      • help arrange financing

☐ Know the specifications of your home/property which can influence price and validate your claims. Write (and have duplicated) a typed fact sheet listing:
    ___ square footage of living space
    ___ number/size of rooms ... number of bedrooms
    ___ number/type of bathrooms
    ___ roofing/siding material
    ___ type of heating/cooling
    ___ water source
    ___ waste disposal system
    ___ type of foundation/basement
    ___ size of lot
    ___ age/style/type of house
    ___ date of available occupancy

☐ List desirable features of home; look at local newspaper ads to see what selling points are stressed.
    ___ fully landscaped
    ___ porch/screened
    ___ brick/cedar shingles
    ___ privacy/view/large backyard
    ___ new/country kitchen
    ___ woodburning fireplace
    ___ finished attic/basement
    ___ fully insulated/storm windows/Thermopane windows

☐ Be prepared to produce records to show potential buyers useful facts and figures:
    ___ annual taxes/assessments (school/property)
    ___ heating/cooling/utility bills for last two years

___ appraisal (if you had one done)

___ major improvements with receipts

___ zoning restrictions

☐ Set asking price with a 5 to 10 percent mark-up to allow room for negotiation. Use as a guideline:

___ current asking/selling prices of comparable homes in area

___ estimates from real-estate agents (even if you don't hire one)

___ updated information from tax assessor

___ local title insurance company estimate (check fee)

___ a professional appraiser (check fee)

☐ Decide which items will be sold with the house and which you are willing to negotiate on as part of the sale price:

___ chandeliers

___ storms/screens

___ washer/dryer

___ portable dishwasher

___ refrigerator/stove

___ carpeting/draperies/blinds/shades

___ lawn equipment/snow blower

___ furniture/shelves

___ TV antenna/rotor

☐ Research availability of financing to qualified buyers; consider if it is to your advantage to act as lender (if you can). Look over your mortgage agreement; find out how your bank/ lending institution works out financial arrangements for paying out mortgage.

___ Is there a penalty payment because you will be paying bank loan ahead of agreed schedule?

___ Will lender waive penalty if buyer gets loan from them?

___ Can buyer assume your mortgage? Under what conditions?

___ Will you have to pay a fee (points) charged by lender if buyer uses FHA or VA mortgage with lower interest rates?

☐ Assemble necessary papers for the sale:

___ deed to property/survey map

___ easements/riparian rights

___ homeowner's insurance policy

___ mortgage agreement

___ tax statements

___ improvement loans/fuel bill statement

☐ When you and prospective buyer agree on a sale price, look for a written offer, a sizable deposit (down payment) and a written contract.

☐ Have your own lawyer examine the sales contract/purchase agreement; check conditions which must be met before sale can be completed. Find out circumstances which allow you/prospective buyer to cancel without penalty.

☐ Continue to show house with the understanding that the sale is contingent on the buyer getting financing within specified time.

☐ See "Things to Do Before the Closing," page 59.

# ✓ Things to Do Before You Rent Out/ Sublet/Swap Your Home

☐ Check out your legal right to rent/sublet/swap home.

☐ Find out if your home, belongings, and car will be protected under your insurance coverage, if you need to make special provisions.

☐ Check going rates in your area for a fair rental charge plus security deposit. Keep in mind:

___ length of stay
___ number of people your home sleeps
___ your furnishings
___ what amenities will be available
___ nearness to recreational facilities

☐ Find potential renters/swappers through:

___ personal referrals
___ university housing offices
___ local corporations relocation office
___ notices on community bulletin boards
___ ads in classified pages of local paper
___ home exchange services
___ rental broker (read contract carefully before you sign)

☐ Check references thoroughly.

☐ Set clear conditions; write up an agreement.

___ specific dates for arrival and departure
___ amount of rent/security deposit
___ payment schedule
___ how breakage/damage will be worked out
___ arrangement for using telephone
___ how utility costs will be handled
___ number of occupants
___ if children/pets/smoking are allowed
___ household necessities you will provide
___ what services are included

- cleaning
- parking
- lawn care

- trash/snow removal
- routine repairs (what this covers)
- window washing

___ house-tending chores (if any)

_____ amenities for use

- car/boat
- bicycles
- stereo
- TV/radio
- records/tapes

- recreational facilities
- sauna/hot tub
- toys
- firewood
- barbecue

### Before Renter/Swapper Arrives

☐ Make sure household equipment is in working order; arrange for necessary repairs; put screens and storms in place.

☐ Store or lock up heirlooms, antiques and fragile items; bring household inventory up to date; place valuables and important papers in safe deposit box.

☐ Double-check that you have provided sufficient/agreed-upon necessities, including adequate closet and drawer space.

☐ Clean house thoroughly. Leave an assortment of staples for vacation renter; stock refrigerator if you and swapper agreed.

☐ Make extra set of keys if needed.

☐ Assemble materials for convenience of renter/swapper.

_____ copies of pertinent local ordinances
_____ town beach stickers/club membership
_____ area maps
_____ information on shopping/restaurants/sightseeing/public recreational facilities/upcoming events
_____ appliance booklets
_____ directions on care/use of your home

- how heating/cooling systems work
- garbage collection
- pet/plant/lawn care
- location of fuse box or circuit breakers/fire extinguishers/security devices/water shut-off/extra linens
- locking up home
- where to pick up/leave keys

☐ Post important telephone numbers.

_____ where you can be reached
_____ another person responsible for decisions
_____ repair-service people
_____ local doctor/baby-sitter
_____ neighbor(s)

# Your Finances and Records

- ☐ **List of Assets and Liabilities**

- ☐ **Checklist for Making a Will**

- ☐ **Checklist for Updating a Will**

- ☐ **Safe Deposit Box List**

- ☐ **Life Insurance Checklist**

- ☐ **Home Insurance Checklist**

- ☐ **Tax-Time Checklist**

- ☐ **Things to Do After a Death in the Family**

- ☐ **Household Records List**

- ☐ **College Financial Aid Checklist**

# List of Assets and Liabilities

Update your list annually; keep a dated copy in your home records file; note what assets are held jointly/what is owned separately and by whom.

## What You Own

Use current market values in estimating your dollar figures.

☐ real estate

   ___ home(s)
   ___ land
   ___ out-of-state holdings
   ___ mortgage equity
   ___ _____
   ___ _____

☐ cash in bank

   ___ savings accounts
   ___ checking account funds
   ___ _____

☐ personal life insurance policies (cash surrender value)

☐ employee benefits

   ___ pension(s)
   ___ profit-sharing
   ___ _____
   ___ _____

☐ private retirement account

☐ securities

   ___ government savings bonds
   ___ stocks
   ___ _____

   ___ _____
   ___ _____

☐ business interests/ equipment

☐ money owed you

   ___ rebates/refunds
   ___ promissory notes
   ___ bills outstanding
   ___ rent
   ___ royalties
   ___ shares in trust fund(s)
   ___ judgments

☐ vehicle(s)

   ___ car(s)
   ___ boat
   ___ motorcycle
   ___ _____

☐ personal effects

   ___ heirlooms/antiques
   ___ home furnishings/ household goods and appliances
   ___ hobby and sports equipment
   ___ art/books/coin/stamp collections
   ___ jewelry/furs/wearing apparel
   ___ pets

☐ miscellaneous

   ___ _____
   ___ _____

## What You Owe

☐ bills

   ___ goods (including store/ credit card debts)
   ___ services (doctor/school fees, etc.)

☐ mortgage(s) (balance due)

☐ loans

   ___ installment credit
   ___ insurance policy
   ___ personal
   ___ _____

☐ taxes

   ___ income
   ___ property
   ___ _____

☐ pledges to charity

☐ claims against your estate

   ___ liens on property
   ___ court-ordered judgments
   ___ pending lawsuit(s)

☐ other

# ✔ Checklist for Making a Will

- If you don't have a will, the state will decide what happens to your property and minor children. Get professional help to write one.

☐ Have you examined your assets and liabilities to find out your net worth?

☐ Do you know the latest IRS regulations relating to estate taxes? State regulations?

☐ Do you have assets that can pass directly to your beneficiaries outside your will to take care of immediate living expenses?

    ___ jointly owned personal and/or real property

    ___ life insurance payable to named beneficiary

    ___ bearer bonds

    ___ employee benefits (annuities/pensions/profit-sharing plan)

    ___ certain trusts

☐ Have you named executor(s)? Is the person(s) likely to outlive you? Have you named alternates?

☐ Have you considered those you want to protect:

    ___ spouse

    ___ minor children/married children

    ___ sick or disabled family member

    ___ grandchildren

    ___ other relatives

    ___ friends

☐ Have you decided who you will name as guardian/trustee for your minor children? Have you named an alternate? Do you want to protect your minor children by:

    ___ leaving the bulk of your estate in trust, stating at what ages and in what amounts you want the principal to be distributed

    ___ providing for their education

    ___ placing limits on the guardian/trustee

    ___ waiving the requirement of posting bond for guardian/trustee

☐ Are there any special situations that might create problems if not dealt with clearly in your will? Do you need expert advice on distributing your assets in regard to:

    ___ divorce/children of former marriage/ex-spouse

    ___ premarital agreement/remarriage

    ___ property ownership in other state(s)

    ___ passing assets outside the will/direct disposition

    ___ use of gifts/trusts

    ___ personal bequests

    ___ different needs of children/non-equal division

    ___ disinheriting someone

## Things to Remember

☐ Laws vary widely from state to state and change frequently; use a lawyer/tax specialist who is expert in your state's tax and estate laws.

☐ Find ways to make your will flexible for future situations such as the effect of inflation; see if you can use percentages rather than dollar amounts unless making small bequests.

☐ Find out how you can pay the executor fees on your estate: time/percentage/fixed fee. Contact your executor(s) and tell him of your arrangements.

☐ Give exact names and current addresses of all those named in your will (executor/guardian/ trustee/beneficiaries).

☐ Remember to review your will annually; send copy to executor(s) and keep original will with your lawyer or banker (in some states safe deposit box is sealed upon death); let your family know where original is, in your letter of instruction.

## Letter of Instruction

This is not a legal document but it provides vital information for your family.

☐ List people to notify with telephone number/relationship.

☐ List your advisors with telephone number/address:

___ clergyperson

___ executor/lawyer/trustee/banker

___ accountant

___ insurance agent/stock broker

___ employment benefits coordinator

☐ Give details of funeral/burial arrangements. Be sure to include:

___ location of cemetery plot/deed

___ membership certificate of memorial society/lodge

___ bequeathal affidavit (donation of body to science)

___ preference for the disposal of remains (burial/cremation/donation to medical science)

___ type of funeral service

___ where to send memorial gifts/donations

☐ List survivor benefits that are passed outside the will; give amounts due and data required to claim them.

☐ Note location of all important documents. Refer to Household Records List and Safe Deposit Box List.

☐ Note policy numbers of all insurance, coverage amounts and premium due dates.

☐ Review letter of instruction annually; keep copy in your household records file and safe deposit box. (Do not keep original in box because in some states it is sealed at time of death.)

# ✓ Checklist for Updating a Will

☐ When was the last time you reviewed your will? Is it time for its periodic check?

☐ Do you want to use the same attorney? Is that attorney available?

☐ Has your legal residence changed? Have you moved to a different state where laws are different?

☐ Are there any changes in family status (births, deaths, marriage, divorce, your own remarriage)?

☐ Have you changed your mind about any of the beneficiaries?

☐ Has your taxable estate changed? Do you have more or fewer assets?

☐ Do you still want to leave the same monetary amounts and/or personal bequests?

☐ Are you giving away something you don't own any more?

☐ Are the executor/executrix and/or your children's guardian still available and willing to take on the responsibility?

☐ Have state or federal estate and tax laws changed in any way that could affect your will?

☐ Was your will drafted before the Tax Reform Act of 1976 became effective? Do you know how jointly owned property is now treated?

☐ If you have acquired a business interest, have you provided for its disposition at your death? Are your partnership papers in order?

☐ Do you have any new thoughts on estate planning that suggest changes in your will?

☐ Does your letter of instruction also require updating? Is it in agreement with the terms of your will?

☐ Do you need to review any trusts?

☐ Can a codicil added to the will do the job? Does it identify the will being amended and confirm the portions that it does not change? Does it meet the same legal requirements as your will?

☐ Is it easier to have a new will drawn up because of the number of changes?

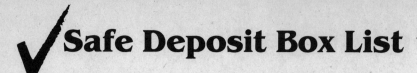

# Safe Deposit Box List

Assign a deputy (preferably a younger person) to have access to your safe deposit box for emergency purposes.

## Original Documents

☐ Personal

    ____ birth certificates
    ____ marriage certificates
    ____ death certificates
    ____ divorce/separation decrees/property settlements
    ____ adoption/custody papers
    ____ citizenship papers
    ____ car/boat title papers
    ____ household inventory (dated)
    ____ appraisals
    ____ _____
    ____ _____

☐ Investments

    ____ stock certificates
    ____ bonds
    ____ saving certificates
    ____ _____
    ____ _____
    ____ _____

☐ Business

    ____ professional licenses
    ____ patents/copyrights
    ____ partnership/corporation agreements/insurance
    ____ certificates of doing business
    ____ _____

____ _____

____ _____

☐ Real Estate

    ____ deeds/title papers/engineering report/survey
    ____ property purchase/sales contracts
    ____ mortgages
    ____ leases
    ____ records of home improvements
    ____ _____

☐ Valuables

    ____ jewelry
    ____ gold/silver
    ____ coins/stamps
    ____ _____
    ____ _____

## Important Copies (indicate location of originals)

____ will with letter of instruction
____ cemetery plot deed
____ trust agreement(s)
____ list of insurance policies
____ list of bank accounts
____ _____
____ _____

# ✓Life Insurance Checklist

☐ Evaluate who needs protection:

    ____ spouse, working/nonworking
    ____ children, ages
    ____ parents, other living relatives
    ____ business partner(s)
    ____ _____

☐ Estimate how much income your beneficiaries would need, and for how long. Note benefits they will receive from other sources (social security, veteran's administration, other insurance, investment income monies).

☐ Figure out the amount of money you can afford to pay for life insurance on a monthly/annual basis.

☐ Check other policies you have that may carry life insurance benefits (employer group life, mortgage/other loan rider).

☐ Be clear about the purpose you want your individual life policy to serve so you can evaluate which types of coverage would best suit your short- and long-range needs.

## Basic Types of Coverage

☐ Term Insurance

    ____ has no cash value
    ____ pays benefits if death occurs during term
    ____ premiums rise as you grow older and renew policy at end of each term
    ____ low premiums

☐ Whole (Straight) Life Insurance

    ____ has cash value/savings benefit
    ____ protection for life without increase in premium
    ____ you can collect the accumulated cash value in lump sum if you surrender the policy

☐ Endowment Insurance

    ____ high cash value and premiums
    ____ limited protection with savings plan

**Before you Buy**

☐ Term

___ How many years does the term cover?
___ At what rate does premium rise each term?
___ Is the policy automatically renewable after the term expiration date? Even if your health changes?
___ Can policy be converted to whole life insurance at a later time without having to take a medical exam?

☐ Whole

___ Are payments made until death or are they limited to a set number of years? Is the price difference worth it to you?
___ How much do you forfeit if you cash in the policy before it is paid in full?
___ What is the rate of interest if you borrow against the cash value?
___ Is this a participating insurance company that pays dividends to its policy holders?
___ Can you use dividends toward premium payments or to buy more insurance? Can you take them out in cash or leave them in an interest-bearing account?
___ Does policy include a waiver of premium if illness/accident prevents you from working?
___ How are benefits to be paid on death? Lump sum, payments over a specified period, reinvestment in an annuity?

☐ Endowment

___ Does the policy pay the full amount in a lump sum or on an income basis after it matures?
___ For what length of time does the policy offer protection?

*Things to Remember*

• You save money if you can pay premiums annually.

• Find out if your group life insurance can be converted to an individual policy.

• Shop around and consider the range of options available to you. Compare costs of similar coverage offered by private insurance companies doing business in your state, savings banks, group plans.

# ✓ Home Insurance Checklist

☐ When was your home/property last appraised? Do you know its current replacement cost?

☐ Are you aware that your home must be insured for at least 80 percent of its replacement cost for you to receive full payment for any loss, partial or total?

☐ Is your household inventory list up to date? Do you know the current value of the contents of your home?

☐ Have you looked at how the dwelling insurance you carry affects other property coverage? Given the stated amount on your policy, are you protected if:

   \_\_\_\_ household contents are valued at 50 percent of dwelling insurance
   \_\_\_\_ other structures (such as a garage) are valued at 10 percent
   \_\_\_\_ additional living expenses are figured at 20 percent (when house cannot be occupied due to physical damage)

☐ Do you know which "perils" are/are not covered in your policy?

☐ What is the liability coverage provided under your homeowner's policy? In case of a claim against you, what are your stated limits for:

   \_\_\_\_ personal liability (if a visitor to your property is hurt, or you, a member of your family causes accidental damage to someone else's property)
   \_\_\_\_ medical payments (regardless of fault) for minor injuries on your property or for you/your family in accidents that occur on someone else's property

**Before You Buy**

☐ Evaluate if you want or need:

   \_\_\_\_ to insure your home at full or 80 percent value
   \_\_\_\_ to revise your liability amount
   \_\_\_\_ a personal property floater

    • What is the maximum amount you can receive on any one unscheduled article?
    • Can you increase the amount for personal property stated on your policy?

☐ Find out if your insurance stays in effect if you and your family are away from home more than thirty days.

☐ Investigate ways to reduce your costs.

   \_\_\_\_ Can you raise your deductibles?
   \_\_\_\_ What form of peril coverage do you need?
   \_\_\_\_ Have you installed approved fire/burglar alarm systems?
   \_\_\_\_ Have you looked at homeowner package policies?
   \_\_\_\_ Does the insurance carrier for your car offer a combined coverage rate?

☐ Check out special forms of coverage available:

   \_\_\_\_ if you rent a house or apartment
   \_\_\_\_ if you own a condo or live in a mobile home
   \_\_\_\_ if there are special conditions in your area such as floods/earthquakes

☐ Before you sign, read the fine print; make sure you understand all the terms/conditions of the policy.

# ✓ Tax-Time Checklist

- Be sure to check the latest IRS rulings to get the best tax benefits for you.

☐ Do you know the best way to file? Find out:

  ___ your filing status for current maximum benefit

  ___ criteria for claiming dependents

  ___ personal exemptions to which you are entitled

  ___ eligibility requirements/check conditions and special forms needed for figuring various tax items

  ___ if you can benefit from the income averaging method

☐ Do you have all the necessary forms and statements (such as W-2, 1099) that should be sent to you by January 31?

☐ Do your personal ongoing records show your other sources of income?

  ___ capital gains/losses

  ___ estates/trusts

  ___ _____

  ___ _____

  ___ rents

  ___ alimony received

  ___ _____

  ___ _____

☐ Can you back up deductions and adjustments you plan to claim on your tax return?

  ___ moving expenses

  ___ alimony paid (by divorce decree)

  ___ disability income

___ non-reimbursed employee expenses

___ retirement plan contributions (IRA, Keogh)

___ _____

___ _____

☐ Is it worthwhile for you to itemize deductions and have you kept accurate records of such items?

  ___ medical/dental expenses (including insurance premiums and transportation)

  ___ taxes paid on real estate/general sales tax/other

  ___ charity contributions cash and noncash value (to qualified organizations)

  ___ interest on loans

    - mortgages
    - credit cards/charges
    - personal
    - business
    - _____
    - _____

  ___ employment expenses
    - union dues
    - malpractice insurance
    - professional periodical subscriptions
    - _____
    - _____

  ___ operating expenses of office in your home (used regularly and exclusively)
    - rent
    - utilities
    - _____
    - _____

  ___ casualty and theft losses not recovered through insurance

___ _____

___ _____

___ _____

☐ Do you know what tax credits you may be qualified to receive?

    ___ political contributions (note maximum allowancc)

    ___ child/disabled dependent care

    ___ elderly (with specified limits)

    ___ residential energy conservation

    ___ foreign income tax paid

    ___ investments on certain new/used business equipment or property

    ___ if your adjusted gross income is less than the stated minimum

    ___ _____

    ___ _____

### Things to Remember

☐ If your return is audited and you disagree with the changes proposed by the examiner, you have the right to appeal within the IRS (30 day limit) or go directly to the U.S. courts.

☐ You can get an automatic two-month time extension by filling out form, but you must still send your check to the IRS by April 15 for taxes you figure are due.

☐ If you underestimate taxes due, you owe the government interest; you will also have to pay a penalty if you underestimate by more than 10 percent.

☐ If you need to correct a return, you are able to do it up to three years later.

☐ Look for refund, if you are due one, within ten weeks after filing; if you do not receive it, call IRS office or write the Service Center where you filed, giving your name/address/social security number.

### Before You Mail the Return

- Have you checked that all income deductions, credits and tax items are on the correct lines?

- Have you included all necessary dated signatures (yours/spouse)?

- Have you written your social security number on your check or money order? On the return?

- Are all the necessary forms attached? Are supplementary schedules filled out/attached?

- Have you made copies for your files?

- Have you enclosed your check made out for the right amount and signed it?

# ✓ Things to Do After a Death in the Family

### Take Care of Funeral Arrangements

☐ Check home file for letter of instruction stating funeral preferences, and where all important personal and financial records can be found.

☐ Call funeral home to set exact date, time and place of funeral. Find out prices and what is/is not included in the funeral arrangement.

☐ Make sure that the funeral director has all the necessary information and documents to make arrangements for:

___ certified copies of death certificate (10–12 copies)
___ obituary notices
___ cemetery burial (plot deed)
___ donation to science (bequeathal affidavit)
___ cremation
___ limousine(s)
___ type of casket/urn
___ flowers/music/reception area/guest book

☐ Notify relatives, friends, employer, business associates, membership organizations of time and place of funeral.

☐ Contact clergyperson to conduct services and arrange for eulogist, pall bearers.

☐ Have family and close friends provide food and hospitality for the next few days. Ask them to manage the household and to keep records of all persons giving condolences (calls, cards, flowers, gifts) for later notes of appreciation; have them contact out-of-town relatives, friends and arrange child care, if necessary.

### Take Care of Legal Arrangements

☐ Consult attorney who holds the original will. The attorney will contact the executor(s) and take necessary legal steps to validate the will and have the court empower the executor(s) to conduct the business of the estate.

☐ Give copies of certified death certificates and any bills incurred for funeral expenses to executor.

☐ Review death benefits and you or executor can file claims for them; ask same sources about income benefits for survivors, what documents are needed, what payout options are. Contact:

    ___ social security office
    ___ Veteran's Administration
    ___ employer benefits coordinator
    ___ labor union/fraternal/professional/religious organizations

☐ If you are named executor/executrix, note the following:

## What Executor Does

___ notifies bank (accounts may be closed, safe deposit box sealed)

___ arranges for IRS representative to be present for opening of box and accounting of contents for tax purposes

___ keeps copy of accounting list

___ reopens bank account under his name as executor for the estate of the deceased

___ checks if credit life insurance covered major loans

___ receives all bills/tax statements and pays after validating them as just claims

    • funeral expenses (or reimbursement)
    • hospital/doctor bills of deceased
    • personal debts of deceased
    • executor/attorney/accountant fees

___ arranges transfers of title when necessary (bank and brokerage accounts)

___ collects any monies due the estate

    • annuities/dividends
    • partnership/corporate business income

___ carries out agreements signed by deceased

    • partnership/corporate insurance policies
    • buy-out agreements
    • sell or maintain present business

___ obtains appraisal of assets if necessary

___ conducts business of the estate until it is disposed of satisfactorily.

    • files estate tax return
    • arranges proper distribution of assets to rightful heirs after tax claims have been settled and required legal time has passed

# ✔ Household Records List

## Personal

___ education records
     (diplomas/transcripts/awards)
___ religious records (baptismal/communion)
___ passports
___ family health records

___ certified copy of birth certificate(s)
___ copy of will(s) with letter(s) of instruction
___ inventory of safe deposit box contents (dated)
___ pet licenses/immunization certificates
___ copy of trust(s) agreements

## Employment

___ contracts
___ social security card stubs/benefits data
___ pension/profit-sharing plans/annuities

___ health insurance benefits
___ letters of recommendation
___ résumé (dated)

## Household

___ appliance manuals/warranties
___ copy of household inventory (dated)
___ copy of any appraisals

## Financial

___ unpaid bills
___ paid bill receipts (for current tax year)
___ current back statements/cancelled checks (for current tax year)
___ bank passbooks/checkbooks
___ list of credit card accounts by issuer/number/renewal dates/insurance
     for them/where to call if lost
___ retail credit/installment loan contracts
___ promissory notes
___ list of securities by issuer/certificate number
___ purchase/sales statements of stocks
___ insurance policies/list of premium due dates
___ record of insurance claims and payments

## Taxes

___ tax assessment notices
___ tax receipts
___ income tax working papers
___ copies of past five years of income tax returns (with canceled checks/
     paid receipts)
___ federal gift tax returns

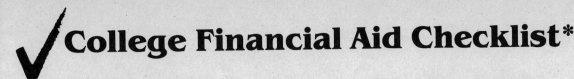

# College Financial Aid Checklist*

## Things to Remember

- Almost all schools offer packages made up of different types of financial aid:

  ____ scholarship or grant (no repayment required)

  ____ loan (repayment with interest after school)

  ____ student work-study program

- Eligibility for aid is not based on family income alone. Demonstrated need is calculated. (This is the difference between what it costs to attend a particular college—including tuition, board, books, travel—and how much the family can afford to pay.)

- You may be eligible for different amounts of aid at different colleges because the amount that the family can be expected to contribute stays the same, but the demonstrated need may change with more expensive schools.

- Government-sponsored loans usually offer the lowest rates and most flexible repayment terms.

## Things to Do

☐ Check with high school guidance counselor for help in finding out about private, state and federal programs available and on how to apply for financial aid. Investigate:

  ____ private funding

  - foundations/corporations

  - professional groups/unions

  - religious organizations

  - community service groups (cultural/civic/fraternal)

  - special interest groups

  ____ government funds

  - Basic Educational Opportunity Grant (BEOG)

  - state scholarships

  - student loans/parent loans

  - College Work-Study program (CWS)

  - Supplemental Education Opportunity Grant program (SEOG)

☐ Find out the limits on the total amount of government aid you can receive as an undergraduate. Ask:

  ____ limits on loans for you/your parents for one year/total undergraduate schooling

  ____ interest rate on loans

  ____ when loan repayments start/deferment policy

  ____ repayment period/prepayment penalties

  ____ maximum amounts listed for grants for the year

## Applying for Aid

☐ Write to the financial aid office at the same time you write for college applications from admissions office (early in senior high school year). Get information:

  ____ the total cost of college for one year

  ____ if school participates in federal aid program

  ____ which forms you must fill out/where to get them and send them

  ____ deadlines for filing all forms/applications

*Latest changes in eligibility/amounts usually can be ascertained through a college finanacial aid office.

- [ ] Arrange to take the SAT (Scholastic Aptitude Test) if scores are required for scholarship applications.

- [ ] Fill out the proper financial aid forms and see if an official copy of your tax return is requested. You will need to gather your financial information from:

  ___ latest tax return

  ___ W-2 forms

  ___ current bank statements

  ___ mortgage statements

  ___ listed assets

  ___ nontaxable income

- [ ] Send completed form to analysis center noting any drastic income changes (such as job loss/disability) and circumstances which use up family funds (another child at college).

- [ ] Clearly indicate on form the colleges to which you wish all information and data sent.

- [ ] Expect a SER (Student Eligibility Report) in four to six weeks. (It is the official notification of your eligibility index number. The lower the number the higher the amount of aid you will be awarded.)

- [ ] Contact Basic Grants, P. O. Box T, Iowa City, Iowa 52243, if you don't receive your SER by six weeks after you've sent in your financial form.

- [ ] Send your SER to the financial aid office at the school you will be attending. If you are considering more than one school, make copies of your SER and send one to each school.

- [ ] Compare financial aid packages sent from each college and choose one which best suits your financial needs.

- [ ] Send the college you plan to attend your original SER.

- [ ] Apply for a student loan if you need more funds in order to attend the college. Go to your local bank and get the loan application; fill out your part and the college will certify your enrollment and supply other information necessary to process the loan.

- [ ] Register at school and go to the financial aid office to find out the school's procedures to receive all your loans/grants/and work-study awards.

- [ ] Note that your financial aid package lasts for one academic year; you must reapply each year. (You may not qualify for certain aid one year but be eligible the next.)

# Keeping Your Home in Shape

- ☐ Things to Do Before You Move
- ☐ Things to Do on Moving Day
- ☐ Things to Do After Moving In
- ☐ Checklist for Dealing with a Contractor
- ☐ Checklist for Filing Homeowner's Insurance Claim
- ☐ Household Inventory List
- ☐ Do-It-Yourself Painting Checklist
- ☐ Basic Repair Tools List
- ☐ List to Ready Your House for Winter
- ☐ Summerizing Your Home Checklist
- ☐ Home Security Checklist

 # Things to Do Before You Move

### A Month Before

☐ Sell or give away what you don't want. Hold a tag sale or donate to charitable resale organization.

☐ Get written appraisals for items of extraordinary value that movers will carry.

☐ Get written estimates of costs from movers. Discuss full services, valuable items, insurance, extra charges and method of payment such as certified check. Ask to have extra wardrobe cartons, lamp cartons, mirror cartons, barrels brought on moving day in case you need them.

☐ If planning to move yourself, be sure a rented vehicle is available and properly licensed; obtain packing materials, rent pads; line up help for moving day, take special care with insurance.

☐ If necessary, make hotel reservations and note to reconfirm.

☐ Notify of your change of address:

    ___ post office
    ___ insurance companies
    ___ charge-account stores
    ___ banks
    ___ credit-card firms
    ___ IRS
    ___ social security (only necessary if you receive checks)
    ___ Department of Motor Vehicles
    ___ magazine/newspaper, mail delivery
    ___ friends
    ___ business associates

☐ Transfer records:

    ___ schools
    ___ medical (doctor/druggist/dentist/veterinarian)
    ___ insurance companies
    ___ banks
    ___ lawyer

☐ Open bank account, rent safe-deposit box in new location.

☐ Start collecting newspapers and packing cartons; buy felt markers, masking tape, notebook.

☐ Update your household inventory list.

☐ Seal cartons as you go along; number and identify what is in them. Pack easiest nonbreakable items first; place heaviest items at bottom; put similar things together. Keep numbered master list of cartons/contents.

### Two Weeks Before

☐ Make pick-ups from cleaners, repair people; collect and return borrowed items.

☐ Stop services on moving day; notify service offices of new address and check for refunds:

    ___ gas
    ___ electric
    ___ water
    ___ telephone
    ___ garbage collection
    ___ newspaper delivery
    ___ laundry delivery
    ___ _____
    ___ _____

☐ Arrange start-up of utility- and-home-delivery services at new address.

☐ If you plan to move heavy appliances such as a gas dryer, contact appropriate company to disconnect and ready it for moving day.

☐ If you are an apartment dweller, reserve elevator for day and time of move.

## One Week Before

☐ Get certified check to pay movers; where applicable, close bank accounts.

☐ Arrange for care of young children and pets on moving day.

☐ Take down curtains, rods, shelves, TV antenna.

☐ Put things you will need right away in new home in specially marked carton(s):

____ soap
____ towels
____ toilet tissues/paper towels
____ cleaning supplies/rags (Do not ship combustible cleaning fluids.)
____ large trash bags
____ light bulbs
____ flashlight/candles/safety matches
____ fuses
____ clock
____ pan/pot for cooking
____ eating utensils
____ paper cups/plates
____ coffee, tea
____ first aid

____ _____
____ _____

☐ Start packing suitcases you can live out of for first day in new home; set aside those items you want to take in your car; mark cartons clearly and try to keep them separate.

☐ Notify police if house will be left vacant.

## One Day Before

☐ Clean refrigerator/freezer, oven/range.

☐ Give away or throw out all remaining perishable food items except those needed for breakfast and trip.

☐ Give away or throw out all household flammable products.

☐ Finish packing personal belongings. Carry with you:

____ valuables in strongbox (papers/jewelry)
____ cash
____ personal/traveler's checks
____ emergency telephone numbers
____ master packing list
____ household inventory list

____ _____
____ _____

____ _____

☐ Plan on simple breakfast, paper plates, no cooking; prepare food/snacks for trip.

☐ Seal and label all remaining cartons.

# Things to Do on Moving Day

## At Old Address

- Strip beds and finish any last-minute chores. Mark fragile items that need special attention.

- Be present or have someone else responsible on the premises when the mover arrives. S/he should be able to answer any questions or make any necessary decisions.

- Before loading, get driver's name, main van line office telephone number, and vehicle license number.

- Point out any fragile items; ask about extra insurance and/or special handling; have any items of extraordinary value written separately on bill of lading with value to be covered.

- Check mover's inventory/bill of lading and appraisal of the condition of your furniture; count the number of cartons against your numbered master list; straighten out any discrepancies before you and the driver sign it.

- Before signing bill of lading, check that all insurance coverage is indicated; get the cost of extra cartons and crating; check addition; sign and carry your copy with you.

- Before van is closed, look in each room and closet to see if anything has been forgotten.

- Make sure you have all cartons and other items (including jewelry/other valuables) in your car that you wanted to carry with you.

- See that your delivery address is correct; give driver clear directions on how to get to your new home; if possible, give him telephone number where he can reach you or a neighbor; get expected time of his arrival.

- Sweep house clean; close and lock windows, lock house and give keys to appropriate person.

- Where applicable, have utility companies verify that they are turning utilities off.

## At New Address

- See if arrangements have been followed for turning on utilities.

- Be there before delivery time. Decide in advance where you want furniture placed and direct movers accordingly; ask them to put marked cartons in appropriate rooms, out of traffic area.

- Be sure movers reassemble any articles they took apart (bed, piano).

- Check all items against bill of lading to see if furniture, cartons and/or suitcases are obviously damaged or missing; note these in writing on both the driver's and your copy of the inventory/bill of lading before signing delivery receipt.

- Double check total cost figure before turning over payment; note any discrepancies in writing.

# ✓ Things to Do After Moving In

☐ Set aside an accessible, safe place to keep important papers during this interim period.

☐ Note where you want to place telephones; keep track of additional hardware items you need to buy as you set up and unpack.

☐ Get household into running order as quickly as possible. Use whatever stopgap measures are necessary.

  ___ *Bathroom:* Set up for immediate use with shower curtain, toothpaste/brushes, first-aid items, soap, towels, toilet tissue.

  ___ *Kitchen:* Set up work/eating space ... buy refrigerator basics ... organize cabinet space ... put down shelving paper ... unpack staples ... install organizers and hooks ... set out trash baskets/cans.

  ___ *Bedrooms:* Unpack only necessary clothing ... cover windows with sheets for temporary privacy ... plan use of closet space.

  ___ *Living Room:* Arrange sitting area with adequate lighting ... keep full cartons elsewhere.

☐ Alert family members to dangerous, temporary hazards such as poorly lit stairwells, extension cord placement.

☐ Make arrangements, if you haven't already done so, to:

  ___ change locks

  ___ install telephone(s) and other utilities

  ___ install security devices (smoke detector/alarm)

  ___ hook up television/antenna

  ___ start garbage/snow removal service

  ___ start newspaper delivery

☐ Examine each item as you unpack noting any damage. If possible, leave item in original carton. In case of damage, notify agent or mover and request claim form. (You have nine months from date of delivery but try to notify in less than thirty days.)

☐ Live in the home a while before making major decorating decisions. This will give you a clearer idea of family activity centers and needs.

☐ Arrange for estimates for any repairs or carpentry work you may need. Get shelves up quickly so you can clear out cartons of books and bric-a-brac.

☐ Arrange to take care of necessary legalities:

  ___ register car in state/apply for plates

  ___ apply for state driver's license

  ___ notify board of elections/register to vote

  ___ enroll children at school(s)

  ___ arrange for credit at local stores/banks

# ✓ Checklist for Dealing with a Contractor

### Before You Decide

☐ Get recommendations from people in your community who have done business with local contractors; avoid out-of-town companies and door-to-door solicitations.

☐ Interview three contractors/companies; visit office if there is one and ask for references from customers whose work has been completed.

☐ If major building, remodeling or repairs are involved, check contractor's reputation and credit standing with:

___ trade associations (National Home Improvement Council/National Association of Home Builders/National Swimming Pool Institute)

___ community organizations (Chamber of Commerce/Better Business Bureau)

___ dealers at wholesale supply houses. Ask several and see if the same names are recommended.

☐ Call references; try to arrange a meeting with previous customers where you can examine contractor's work; ask if it was finished on time, if any problems arose along the way.

☐ Get several bids on the same job from contractors whose references check out; ask for written estimates based on identical specifications (same sizes, quantity and quality of materials, and labor).

### Before You Sign

☐ Insist on a written contract that is specific. It should include:

___ plans/sketches/specifications for work to be done
___ detailed descriptions of materials to be used.
  • quantities
  • sizes
  • weights
  • brand names
  • grades
  • colors
  • number of coats
___ production schedule with calendar dates for starting and finishing the job
___ payment schedule (including method of payment)
___ cancellation clause
___ penalty clause (if work is unreasonably late)
___ change clause
___ who supplies materials

_____ who secures needed permits/licenses; who pay fees

_____ who hires, pays and has ultimate responsibility for the job if sub-contractors are needed

☐ Make sure you read and understand the entire contract.

    _____ Has contractor included provisions for financing your home-improvement project? (Consider deleting and making your own arrangements.)

    _____ Is contractor willing to post bond to protect against liens on your home if work is sublet?

    _____ Is payment contingent on work adhering to local building codes so you get the necessary permits?

☐ Check out insurance coverage.

    _____ Is work to be done covered by your insurance? (Show contract to your insurance company.)

    _____ Does contractor provide liability and compensation insurance to cover worker injuries and property damages? (Ask for documentation.)

☐ Never allow any work to begin until contract is signed; do not sign until your lawyer has gone over the contract.

## While Work Is Underway

☐ After initial work is done, have city inspector see if it meets standards.

☐ Put requests for changes and cost estimates in writing; make clear that no change is to be made until you have a written estimate and have approved of it in writing.

☐ Avoid getting in the way of workers; if you have complaints or questions, deal directly with the contractor.

☐ Sign no completion certificate until work is completed as agreed.

☐ Pay only after work is actually completed and acceptable to you; do not make final payment until work has passed inspection and any necessary guarantees/warranties are provided.

# ✓ Checklist for Filing Homeowner's Insurance Claim

### For Fire

☐ Contact insurance representative immediately and ask for help:

    ___ how to minimize further damage
    ___ to find temporary living quarters, if needed
    ___ to provide emergency funds
    ___ to cover any necessary increase in living expenses for the time period required to repair or replace premises and/or until loss settlement is made.

☐ Arrange for reasonable, necessary repairs on property (patching roof/boarding windows/electric/plumbing services); keep accurate records of all such expenditures.

☐ Check loss against your household inventory; use any photos and/or records you have kept to help validate your claim on the value of special pieces; list damaged property in detail:

    ___ quantity
    ___ description
    ___ actual cash value
    ___ amount of loss

☐ Submit your signed, sworn statement of loss within sixty days after insurance company requests it. It should include:

    ___ time and cause of loss
    ___ your interest in the property
    ___ other insurance on the property
    ___ copies of receipts for any additional living expenses incurred

☐ Find out if your policy is figured at 80 percent of the full replacement costs of the building. If so, expect insurer to pay the cost of repair or replacement without deduction for depreciation, but not exceeding the amount of your policy.

### For Robbery, Theft, Burglary

☐ Report the crime to the police station in the vicinity as soon as possible; get the complaint report number and name/badge number of officer taking the data, if possible.

☐ Get a copy of this report; fill out any necessary forms and/or pay fees to have the copy sent to you (it may take several weeks). Let the police know if you would be willing to try to identify the robbers from mug shots and to prosecute.

☐ Send copies of sales receipts of stolen articles with copy of police report and number to your insurer. If receipts are not available, other documentation (cancelled checks) is acceptable.

☐ Find out from insurer if you must assert a claim against the owner of the property where the crime occurred or other persons who share in responsibility.

☐ Check if the insurance carrier replaces the item(s) or pays for the replacement cost. It depends on the policy language or the interpretation of the claims adjuster.

☐ If you don't agree with the figure allowance of the claims adjuster, find out the appeals procedure from your insurer/policy.

# ✔ Household Inventory List

- Keep a written room-by-room record and update periodically; keep the list in safe-deposit box and a copy in household file.

- Note model, serial numbers, descriptions. Take photos for each item. Indicate date purchased, how much it cost and current replacement cost. Keep receipts when possible.

## Living Room

- ☐ chairs
    - ___ upholstered
    - ___ occasional
- ☐ sofa/loveseat
- ☐ tables
    - ___ coffee
    - ___ end
    - ___ _____
- ☐ storage wall units
- ☐ bookcases/books
- ☐ objets d'art/antiques
    - ___ _____
    - ___ _____
    - ___ _____
- ☐ piano/organ/bench/stool
- ☐ desk
- ☐ fireplace accessories
    - ___ _____
    - ___ _____
- ☐ carpeting/rugs
- ☐ draperies/blinds
- ☐ television
- ☐ stereo
- ☐ records/tapes
- ☐ mirrors
- ☐ clock
- ☐ lamps
- ☐ wall decorations
    - ___ sconces
    - ___ paintings
    - ___ _____

- ☐ planters
- ☐ _____
- ☐ _____
- ☐ _____
- ☐ _____
- ☐ _____

## Dining Room

- ☐ table
- ☐ chairs
- ☐ sideboard/buffet
- ☐ breakfront/hutch
- ☐ rugs
- ☐ draperies/blinds
- ☐ mirrors
- ☐ serving cart
- ☐ chandelier
- ☐ pictures
- ☐ silver service
- ☐ china/crystal
- ☐ linens
- ☐ _____
- ☐ _____
- ☐ _____
- ☐ _____
- ☐ _____
- ☐ _____

## Den, Family Room, Enclosed Porch

- ☐ wall units/bookcases/books
- ☐ TV/stereo/records/tapes

- ☐ screen projects
- ☐ chairs
    - ___ _____
    - ___ _____
- ☐ tables
    - ___ _____
    - ___ _____
- ☐ sofa bed
- ☐ carpet/rug
- ☐ draperies/blinds
- ☐ desk/accessories
- ☐ mirror/pictures
- ☐ lamps/lighting fixtures
- ☐ fireplace accessories
- ☐ bar/accessories/stock
- ☐ telephone answering device
- ☐ room accessories
    - ___ throw pillows
    - ___ plants
    - ___ _____
    - ___ _____
- ☐ _____
- ☐ _____
- ☐ _____

## Kitchen, Pantry

- ☐ large/small appliances
    - ___ _____
    - ___ _____
    - ___ _____
- ☐ tables
- ☐ chairs/stools
- ☐ lighting fixture(s)

- ☐ cookware
- ☐ glassware/dishes
- ☐ utensils/flatware
- ☐ accessories
- ☐ food/household supplies

## Bathroom

- ☐ accessories
  - ___ scale
  - ___ hamper
  - ___ curtains/rugs
  - ___ lighting/mirror
  - ___ _____
- ☐ vanity/chair
- ☐ small appliances
- ☐ medicine chest contents
- ☐ toilet articles
- ☐ _____
- ☐ _____

## Halls, Foyers

- ☐ tables
- ☐ chairs
- ☐ wall unit(s)
- ☐ rug
- ☐ lighting fixture
- ☐ objets d'art
- ☐ wall decorations
- ☐ umbrella stand/coat tree

## Closets/Storage

- ☐ coat closet
  - ___ rain gear
  - ___ coats/jackets
  - ___ _____
  - ___ _____

## Linen Closet

- ☐ towels
- ☐ sheets/pillowcases

- ☐ tablecloths/napkins
- ☐ _____
- ☐ _____

## Clothing Closets

- ☐ _____
- ☐ _____
- ☐ _____

## Utility Closet

- ☐ housecleaning equipment / supplies
  - ___ vacuum
  - ___ floor polisher
  - ___ iron/board
  - ___ _____
  - ___ _____

## Miscellaneous Storage

- ☐ hobby/sports equipment
  - ___ sewing machine
  - ___ _____
  - ___ _____
- ☐ _____
- ☐ _____

## Bedrooms (list each)

- ☐ beds
  - ___ springs/mattresses
  - ___ frame/headboards
  - ___ pillows/blankets/quilts
- ☐ lighting fixtures
- ☐ radio/clocks
- ☐ tables
  - ___ night
  - ___ dressing
- ☐ chairs
  - ___ _____
  - ___ _____

## Attic

- ☐ trunks
- ☐ out-of-season clothing

- ☐ hobby equipment
- ☐ sports gear
- ☐ _____
- ☐ _____

## Basement

- ☐ washer/dryer
- ☐ dehumidifier
- ☐ house maintenance gear
- ☐ _____
- ☐ _____
- ☐ _____

## Garage, Tool Shed

- ☐ bicycles
- ☐ lawn furniture
- ☐ portable barbecue
- ☐ lawn-maintenance equipment
- ☐ snow-removal equipment
- ☐ power tools/toolbox
- ☐ _____
- ☐ _____

## Personal Belongings

- ☐ jewelry
- ☐ furs
- ☐ clothing
- ☐ sports equipment (if not listed)
- ☐ hobby collections
- ☐ hobby equipment (if not listed)
  - ___ cameras
  - ___ _____
  - ___ _____
- ☐ _____
- ☐ _____
- ☐ _____

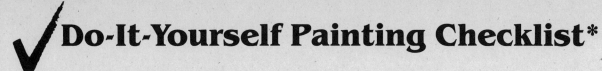

# Do-It-Yourself Painting Checklist*

**Before You Buy Supplies (for painting interior surfaces)**

☐ Note surfaces to be painted:

____ find out which type of paint is preferable for various surfaces (window sills, woodwork, metal radiators)

____ get professional advice on what kind of paint will best adhere (oil or latex)

____ if primer coat is needed, be sure it is compatible with surface and topcoat paint

☐ Figure amount of paint needed:

____ multiply length and height of walls for square footage

____ read instructions on paint can for number of square feet a given quantity of paint covers

____ figure separately the square footage for each color/type of paint

☐ Decide on colors:

____ bring swatches of fabric and sample of flooring to coordinate wall-paint color

____ bring home color chips of paint from store to match colors in room

**Before You Paint**

☐ Prepare surfaces (including trim)

____ scrape off peeling paint

____ sandpaper edges smooth

____ countersink nails

____ fill cracks and holes with spackle/wood filler

____ check if store has all the necessary color paint in stock, noting batch number

____ if using custom-mixed colors, have them mixed from same batch

☐ Get professional help to insure a good paint job:

____ ask dealer to machine-stir all colors

____ get recommended tips on preparing surfaces

____ check drying time

____ get stirrers, painting hat from dealer (usually free)

☐ Find out what equipment is right for your paint job (choose good-quality roller covers/ paint brushes):

____ deep-pile roller for textured surface

____ short-nap roller for high gloss/semigloss

____ medium-nap roller for flat or satin-finish latex

____ synthetic fiber brush for latex/alkyd (oil base)

____ natural bristle for alkyd only

____ sand glossy surfaces lightly

____ spot-prime patched areas

____ vacuum walls or dust with dry mop

____ wash greasy areas with water and detergent

____ apply primer coat if necessary

*See also "Things to Do Before, During and After a Paint Job," page 112.

☐ Check that all furniture, ceiling fixtures and movables are covered with dropcloths or removed from painting area.

☐ Put up masking tape where needed; cover floor with dropcloth.

☐ Ventilate room.

☐ Dampen roller and brush before dipping in paint:

___ water for latex

___ mineral spirits for alkyd

☐ Stir paint thoroughly again.

☐ Transfer paint to clean roller tray without obscuring paint can label.

☐ Recommended painting sequence:

___ ceiling
___ walls
___ window and door trim/sash
___ baseboard
___ doors

## Painting Tips

• Dip only one-third bristle length; tap off excess.

• Never stop in midwall.

• Place roller/brush in plastic bag when taking a break and close bag tightly.

• Clean spills and rollers before paint dries.

• Remove masking tape while paint is still damp.

## Supplies

☐ paints
(flat, semigloss, high gloss)

___ latex (water base)

___ alkyd (oil base)

___ floor enamel

___ epoxy paint

___ wall primer

___ enamel underbody

___ _____

☐ mixing sticks

☐ rollers

___ short-nap

___ medium-nap

☐ roller tray

☐ roller extender pole (6 feet)

☐ brushes

___ trim

___ angled sash

☐ paint thinner

___ mineral spirits (for alkyd)

___ water/soap (for latex)

☐ rubber gloves

☐ 100-watt bulb

☐ dropcloths

☐ newspapers/rags

☐ ladder

☐ screwdriver

☐ yardstick/tape measure

☐ masking tape

☐ sandpaper (finishing grade)

☐ can of latex crack filler

☐ putty knife

☐ razor blade/paint scraper

☐ paint shields

☐ sponge

# ✓ Basic Repair Tools List

☐ steel tape (flexible, 6')

☐ combination square

☐ spirit level (24″)

☐ saws

    ___ carpenter's crosscut

    ___ hacksaw

☐ knives

    ___ putty (stiff/flexible)

    ___ utility (disposable blades)

☐ drills

    ___ push-pull/rotary hand drill with set of bits

    ___ electric drill with set of bits ($\frac{3}{8}$-inch model)

☐ hammer

    ___ carpenter's claw

☐ screwdrivers (large/small)

    ___ flat blade
    ___ Phillips

☐ staple gun/staples

☐ force cup plunger

☐ plumber's snake

☐ plane (standard small)

    ___ block

☐ file

    ___ flat

☐ chisel set ($\frac{1}{2}$″ to 1″)

☐ C-clamp (medium)

☐ vise

☐ pliers

    ___ slip-jointed
    ___ channel-type
    ___ needle-nosed with wire cutter

☐ wrenches

    ___ adjustable crescent (6″, 8″, 10″)
    ___ pipe wrench (medium)
    ___ set of Hex Key wrenches

## Assorted Supplies

☐ fuses

☐ washers

☐ anchors

☐ nuts/bolts

☐ nails/screws

☐ electrical tapes

☐ glues

## Accessories

☐ toolbox

☐ flashlight

☐ ladder

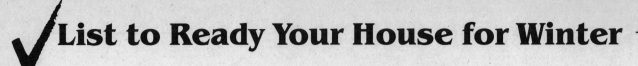

# List to Ready Your House for Winter

### Roof

☐ Look inside unfinished attic for holes or water discoloration stains. Repair/replace damaged or missing tiles, shingles or other roofing material.

☐ Clean gutters/drainpipes of leaves and other debris; tighten gutters; patch rusted-out sections; replace those that cannot be repaired.

### Windows/doors

☐ Apply caulking around all window- and door-frames where there are cracks and worn spots. Scrape off old compound.

☐ Clean storm windows and doors; repair cracked glass; check that storms work properly.

☐ Look for gaps that need weatherstripping; make sure doors/windows fit snugly into frames.

☐ Put rip-free, tight, weatherproof cover on any air conditioner to be left in window.

☐ Clean and store summer awnings/screens.

### Insulation

☐ Check insulation wherever possible in walls, floors, ceilings; look at exposed insulation in attic, basement, crawl spaces to see if damp; replace or add suitable type of insulation, depending on specific area and type of heat.

### Outside Walls

☐ Check house exterior for openings that need caulking; patch cracks in brickwork.

☐ Scrape and touch up peeling areas on outside paint.

### Exposed Plumbing

☐ Note any water pipes that pass through uninsulated areas in or around your home and wrap pipes with insulating tape.

☐ Drain outside water faucets so pipes will not burst from water freezing in them.

### Heating System

☐ Clean heating system according to manufacturer's directions or have serviceperson do it:

___ vacuum ducts in forced-air system

___ change filter and check pilot light in gas-fired system

___ clean burner surfaces on gas or oil heater, electrodes on electric hot-water heater

___ lubricate motors

___ drain hot-water heater and remove sediment from bottom

☐ Make sure chimney flue is free of obstructions; see that damper closes tightly to prevent air leaks.

# ✓ Summerizing Your Home Checklist

☐ Have you inspected house for winter damage? Looked for air leaks around windows and doors? Do you need to caulk or weather-strip to keep out cold air?

☐ Have you examined attic for ventilation or moisture problems? Do you need to reinsulate now? Are attic vents clean and bug-free? Have you cleaned power vents according to manufacturer's instructions?

☐ Have you checked outside of house for cracks and peeling paint? Are you planning to repair and paint to prevent further deterioration?

☐ Have you removed storm windows and stored them, noting which storm belongs to which window/door?

☐ Have you looked over all screens for rips and tears? Have you patched or replaced them? Cleaned and installed them?

☐ Have you taken awnings out of storage? Are they in good condition? Are you planning to install them to protect against summer heat?

☐ Have you cleaned your air-conditioner filter or replaced it, if necessary? Have you stored the cover for window model in a safe, dry place?

☐ Have you arranged for serviceperson to switch off pilot light if you use gas or oil heat?

☐ Have you turned heat thermostats to "off" position?

☐ Have you had fireplace and flue cleaned? Are you keeping damper open for better ventilation? Closed when using air conditioning?

☐ Does basement seem too moist? Have you considered using a special paint or dehumidifier? Have you cleaned your dehumidifier following manufacturer's directions?

☐ Have you finished readying your home for the new season? See "Spring Cleaning Checklist," page 106.

# ✓Home Security Checklist

Is your house/apartment secure from burglars?
Do you need:

____ deadbolt/dropbolt locks with pick-resistant cylinders

____ well-fitted door frames/securely fastened strike plates

____ a wide-angle peephole (180°) in metal or solid wood door

____ door intercom system

____ window reinforcements (metal gates/wire mesh/iron bars/grills)

____ key-operated or pin windows (except for fire-exit windows)

____ polycarbonate plastic to replace plain glass in front-door panels

____ light timers

____ alarm system with displayed notice

____ home safe or closet equipped with deadbolt lock

____ shrubbery trimmed so it does not hide front door

____ security check by police

## DO

____ replace lock cylinders immediately if you lose keys

____ permanently mark your social security number or Operation I.D. number on valuable personal property

____ leave light/timer/radio on when not home

____ hide extra cash where there are many similar items (books/canisters)

____ post notices that items on property have been marked

## DON'T

____ leave keys under doormat/in mailbox

____ put note on door indicating when you will return

____ keep valuables in obvious place such as chest drawer

____ leave ladder against side of house

# Your Household

☐ **The Well-Equipped Kitchen List**

☐ **Checklist for a Sit-Down Dinner Party**

☐ **The Ultimate Marketing List**

☐ **Spring Cleaning Checklist**

☐ **Checklist for Holding a Tag Sale**

☐ **The Well-Stocked Bar List**

☐ **Holiday Chores List**

☐ **Informal Party Checklist**

☐ **Things to Do Before, During and After a Paint Job**

☐ **Basic Medicine Chest List**

☐ **List to Get Ready for a Houseguest**

☐ **Things to Remember When You Redecorate**

☐ **Handy Telephone List**

☐ **Emergency Telephone List**

# ✔ The Well-Equipped-Kitchen List

## Electric Appliances

- [ ] refrigerator
- [ ] freezer
- [ ] dishwasher
- [ ] convection/microwave oven
- [ ] broiler/rotisserie
- [ ] toaster
- [ ] toaster-oven
- [ ] mixer
- [ ] blender
- [ ] food processor
- [ ] juicerator
- [ ] coffeemaker
- [ ] pasta maker
- [ ] can opener
- [ ] knife
- [ ] slicing machine
- [ ] meat grinder
- [ ] deep fryer
- [ ] fry pan
- [ ] hamburger/hot dog grill
- [ ] crock pot
- [ ] waffle iron
- [ ] hot trays
- [ ] ice cream maker
- [ ] peanut butter maker
- [ ] popcorn popper
- [ ] coffee bean grinder
- [ ] cappuccino machine
- [ ] _____
- [ ] _____
- [ ] _____
- [ ] _____

## Utensils

- [ ] salad spinner
- [ ] colander
- [ ] strainers
  - ___ sieve
  - ___ tea
- [ ] vegetable steamer
- [ ] funnel
- [ ] jar lids/seals
- [ ] flour sifter
- [ ] knives
  - ___ paring
  - ___ bread
  - ___ carving
  - ___ grapefruit
  - ___ _____
  - ___ _____
- [ ] knife sharpener
- [ ] bottle/can/jar openers
- [ ] corkscrew
- [ ] kitchen shears
- [ ] ice cream scoop
- [ ] spoons
  - ___ slotted
  - ___ wooden
  - ___ measuring set
  - ___ ladle
  - ___ _____
  - ___ _____
- [ ] poultry pins
- [ ] food scale
- [ ] measuring cups
  - ___ 1-cup
  - ___ 2-cup
  - ___ 1-quart
- [ ] spatulas
- [ ] cooking fork
- [ ] potato masher

- [ ] tongs
- [ ] meat grinder
- [ ] egg beater
- [ ] food mill
- [ ] grater
  - ___ nutmeg
  - ___ chocolate
- [ ] wire whisks
- [ ] mortar and pestle
- [ ] garlic press
- [ ] vegetable brush
- [ ] lemon squeezer
- [ ] pepper mill
- [ ] egg slicer
- [ ] cheese slicer
- [ ] strawberry huller
- [ ] apple corer
- [ ] vegetable peeler
- [ ] shrimp deveiner
- [ ] oyster opener
- [ ] melon-ball cutter
- [ ] rolling pin
- [ ] rubber scrapers
- [ ] cutting boards
- [ ] cookie cutters
- [ ] pastry cloth/cutter
- [ ] wire cake racks
- [ ] molds
- [ ] wooden bowls
- [ ] chopper
- [ ] array of mixing bowls
- [ ] skewers
- [ ] baster
- [ ] cheesecloth
- [ ] thermometers
  - ___ meat

- ___ candy
- ___ deep-fry
- [ ] cake tester
- [ ] _____
- [ ] _____
- [ ] _____
- [ ] _____

## Cookware

- [ ] skillets
  - ___ large cast iron
  - ___ omelet pan
  - ___ _____
  - ___ _____
- [ ] griddle
- [ ] pots/saucepans/covers
  - ___ double boiler
  - ___ enamel
  - ___ _____
  - ___ _____
  - ___ _____
  - ___ _____
- [ ] Dutch oven
- [ ] pressure cooker
- [ ] wok
- [ ] canner
- [ ] teakettle
- [ ] roasting pans/rack
  - ___ _____
  - ___ _____
- [ ] broiling pan
- [ ] fish poacher
- [ ] egg coddler/poacher
- [ ] casseroles
  - ___ _____
  - ___ _____

☐ loaf pans
___ _____
___ _____
___ _____

☐ cake pans
___ _____
___ _____
___ _____

☐ muffin tins
☐ pie dishes
___ quiche pan
___ _____

☐ cookie sheets
☐ _____
☐ _____
☐ _____

## For Serving

☐ trays
___ serving
___ individual
☐ cheese boards
☐ fondue set
☐ chafing dish
☐ punch bowl/cups/ server
☐ coasters
☐ candlesticks/candles
☐ tablecloths/placemats
☐ napkin rings/napkins
☐ salt/pepper servers
☐ condiment dishes
___ _____

☐ vinegar/oil cruets
☐ salad bowl/server
☐ butter dish/paddle

☐ gravy boat/ladle
☐ soup tureen
☐ _____
☐ trivets
☐ pitchers
___ _____
___ _____

☐ baskets
___ bread
___ bun warmer
___ wine server
___ _____

☐ serving utensils
___ vegetable spoons
___ meat fork
___ _____
___ _____
___ _____

☐ carving set/board
☐ serving bowls
___ _____
___ _____
___ _____
___ _____

☐ serving platters
___ _____
___ _____
___ _____

☐ egg cups
☐ ramekins/custard cups
☐ casserole dishes
___ _____
___ _____

☐ soufflé dish
☐ quiche plate
☐ creamer/sugar
☐ cake plates
☐ cake knife/pie cutter
☐ steak knives
☐ fruit knives
☐ fruit bowls
☐ candy/nut dishes
☐ nutcracker
☐ _____
☐ tea/coffee pot/ samovar
☐ tea cozy
☐ mugs
☐ flatware (formal/infor- mal)
___ dinner knives
___ steak knives
___ butter knives
___ fruit knives
___ cocktail forks
___ salad forks
___ dinner forks
___ cake forks
___ teaspoons
___ soup spoons
___ demitasse spoons
___ parfait spoons
___ _____
___ _____

☐ dishes (everyday/for- mal)
___ appetizer
___ salad
___ soup/cereal
___ dinner
___ fruit cup
___ parfait
___ saucers
___ cups
___ _____
___ _____

☐ glassware/stemware
___ juice

___ water
___ wine
___ liqueur

## Equipment

☐ food-storage containers
___ glass jars
___ plastic freezer set
___ juice container
___ _____
___ _____

☐ canister set
☐ spice rack
☐ cutlery rack
☐ pot rack
☐ cookie jar
☐ breadbox
☐ covered cake plate
☐ towel holder
☐ napkin holder
☐ potholders
☐ cookbooks/holder
☐ recipe file
☐ step stool
☐ garbage can
☐ sponges/soap dish
☐ dish drainer/towels
☐ broom/dustpan
☐ mop/pail
☐ _____
☐ kitchen magnets
☐ timer
☐ clock
☐ pad/pencil/telephone
☐ shopping cart
☐ _____
☐ _____
☐ _____

# ✓ Checklist for a Sit-Down Dinner Party

### Menu Planning

☐ Write out menu.

    ____ Have you prepared these menu items before?
    ____ Is it right for the season?
    ____ How many courses are there?
    ____ Will you need kitchen/serving help?
    ____ Is meal well divided between last-minute cooking and ahead-of-time roasting/baking?
    ____ Are there items you can cook and freeze ahead that will thaw well?

☐ Plan timetable; note what portions of the meal you can prepare ahead (a week before, day before, same day).

☐ Check that pots and pans are large enough to accommodate party-size quantities; your oven and range capacity is sufficient to prepare everything according to your timetable.

☐ Note staples required for recipes and make shopping list; look over menu and list wine/liquor/liqueur you want to serve.

☐ Find out if any guest has special diet requirements.

☐ Purchase ingredients:

    ____ appetizer
    ____ soup/salad
    ____ condiments
    ____ main course
    ____ dessert
    ____ hors d'oeuvres

☐ _____

### Table Setting

☐ Double-check serving pieces and place settings against menu items and number of guests. Will you need to rent or borrow anything?

☐ Note which serving pieces/place settings need polishing, cleaning.

☐ Examine all laundered items (napkins, place mats, tablecloths) to make sure they are in good repair, clean and pressed.

☐ Plan table arrangement.

___ Do you want to use place cards?
___ Have you kept smokers and nonsmokers in mind?
___ Will guests be able to see across centerpiece comfortably?
___ Will there be enough room on table for serving dishes?
___ Do you need to order floral centerpiece in advance?

☐ Plan adequate lighting; take into account scented oil and/or dripping candles.

## Serving

☐ Make sure guests will not be distracted by what is going on in kitchen.

☐ If serving roast or fowl, plan to have it carved and served properly.

☐ Arrange for hot trays or cold packs for menu items requiring them.

☐ Map out plan for maximum efficiency given table arrangement and available help.

___ Give clear directions to kitchen help; no confusion over who does what, when.
___ Arrange to have dishes/glasses that will be reused for another course washed and dried immediately.
___ Arrange kitchen counters for setting down extra dishes/serving pieces you will need in consecutive order.
___ Place wine cooler out of path of person serving meal.

___ _____

### *Check Before Guests Arrive*

• Candy/nut dishes are filled.
• Ash trays are clean and set out throughout rooms.
• Extra hand towels are in place in bathroom.
• Fresh fruit bowl is ready.
• Items to be thawed are out of freezer.
• Hors d'oeuvres are ready to serve.
• Cocktails/ice/glasses/coasters are ready to use.
• Water goblets are filled; ice pitcher on table.
• Appetizer is set out or ready to serve.
• Place cards are set.
• Timing of all menu items is on cue.
• Centerpiece and overall setting is complete (including salt/pepper shakers).
• Stereo music is set at background level.
• Lighting is the way you want it; matches are handy to light candles.

# ✔ The Ultimate Marketing List

## Dairy

- ☐ eggs
- ☐ butter/margarine
- ☐ milk
  - ___ skim
  - ___ buttermilk
  - ___ regular
  - ___ _____
  - ___ _____

- ☐ cream
  - ___ light
  - ___ heavy
  - ___ whipped
  - ___ _____
  - ___ _____

- ☐ yogurt
  - ___ fruit
  - ___ _____

- ☐ dips
- ☐ cheese
  - ___ cheddar
  - ___ Swiss
  - ___ _____
  - ___ _____
  - ___ Brie
  - ___ Camembert
  - ___ _____
  - ___ _____
  - ___ cream cheese
  - ___ American
  - ___ _____
  - ___ _____
  - ___ grated Parmesan
  - ___ grated Romano

- ___ _____
- ___ _____

- ☐ sour cream
- ☐ cottage cheese/ricotta
- ☐ farmer cheese
- ☐ horseradish
- ☐ seafood cocktail sauce
- ☐ juice
  - ___ orange
  - ___ grapefruit
  - ___ _____
- ☐ _____
- ☐ _____
- ☐ _____

## Frozen Foods

- ☐ individual dinners
  - ___ _____
  - ___ _____
  - ___ _____

- ☐ vegetables
  - ___ mixed
  - ___ peas
  - ___ spinach
  - ___ _____
  - ___ _____
  - ___ _____

- ☐ potatoes
  - ___ french fries
  - ___ hash brown
  - ___ _____
  - ___ _____

- ☐ pizza
- ☐ ethnic foods
  - ___ egg rolls
  - ___ tacos
  - ___ chopped liver
  - ___ lasagna
  - ___ _____
  - ___ _____
  - ___ _____

- ☐ seafood/fish
  - ___ _____
  - ___ _____
  - ___ _____
  - ___ _____

- ☐ breads/rolls
  - ___ _____
  - ___ _____

- ☐ cookie rolls
- ☐ pies/cakes/cupcakes
- ☐ dessert fruits
- ☐ juices/lemonade
  - ___ _____
  - ___ _____

- ☐ whipped cream
- ☐ ice cream/sherbet
  - ___ _____
- ☐ _____
- ☐ _____
- ☐ _____

- ☐ _____
- ☐ _____

## Deli Department

- ☐ prepared salads
  - ___ potato
  - ___ macaroni
  - ___ coleslaw
  - ___ egg
  - ___ shrimp
  - ___ tuna
  - ___ bean
  - ___ _____
  - ___ _____

- ☐ smoked fish
  - ___ lox
  - ___ whitefish
  - ___ _____
  - ___ _____

- ☐ herring
- ☐ gefilte fish
- ☐ stuffed derma
- ☐ stuffed grape leaves
- ☐ chopped liver
- ☐ salami rolls
  - ___ pepperoni
  - ___ kosher
  - ___ liverwurst
  - ___ bologna

- ☐ ham
  - ___ baked Virginia
  - ___ boiled
  - ___ _____

- ☐ sliced deli meats
  - ___ corned beef
  - ___ pastrami
  - ___ turkey
  - ___ tongue
- ☐ barbecue chicken
- ☐ barbecue spareribs
- ☐ pickles/olives
- ☐ cheese
  - ___ _____
  - ___ _____
- ☐ breads/rolls/bagels
  - ___ rye
- ☐ _____
- ☐ _____
- ☐ _____
- ☐ _____

## Household Items

- ☐ paper goods
  - ___ towels
  - ___ plates/cups
  - ___ napkins
  - ___ straws
  - ___ bath tissues
  - ___ face tissues
  - ___ _____
  - ___ _____
- ☐ bath/face soap
- ☐ foil/wax paper
- ☐ plastic bags
  - ___ trash
  - ___ sandwich
  - ___ freezer
  - ___ _____
- ☐ coffee filters

- ☐ tape
  - ___ masking
  - ___ freezer
  - ___ Scotch
  - ___ _____
- ☐ safety matches
- ☐ lighter fluid
- ☐ candles
- ☐ light bulbs
- ☐ plant food
- ☐ room fresheners
- ☐ kitchen utensils/pots
- ☐ potholders
- ☐ kitchen towels
- ☐ insect/bug killer

## Cleaning Items

- ☐ mop/broom
- ☐ dustcloths
- ☐ brushes
  - ___ toilet
  - ___ scrub
  - ___ vegetable
  - ___ _____
- ☐ sponges/scour pads
- ☐ rubber gloves
- ☐ cleansers
  - ___ oven
  - ___ toilet
  - ___ glass
  - ___ wall
  - ___ sink/tile
  - ___ _____
- ☐ disinfectants/ammonia
- ☐ detergents
  - ___ clothes

- ___ dishes
- ___ floor
- ___ _____
- ___ _____
- ☐ bleach
- ☐ ironing starch
- ☐ fabric softener
- ☐ grease/spot remover
- ☐ polish
  - ___ silver
  - ___ copper/brass
  - ___ furniture
  - ___ shoes
  - ___ _____
- ☐ floor wax/remover

## Baked Goods and Sweets

- ☐ bread
  - ___ white
  - ___ rye
  - ___ pumpernickel
  - ___ whole wheat
- ☐ rolls/muffins
  - ___ hamburger
  - ___ corn
  - ___ _____
  - ___ _____
- ☐ cake
  - ___ _____
  - ___ _____
  - ___ _____
  - ___ _____
- ☐ pie
  - ___ _____

- ___ _____
- ___ _____ ___
- ☐ donuts
- ☐ cookies
  - ___ _____
  - ___ _____
- ☐ crackers
  - ___ _____
  - ___ _____
  - ___ _____
- ☐ pretzels
- ☐ chips
  - ___ potato
  - ___ corn
- ☐ _____
- ☐ _____
- ☐ _____
- ☐ chocolate
  - ___ milk
  - ___ bittersweet
  - ___ _____
  - ___ _____
  - ___ _____
- ☐ mints
- ☐ candy bars
- ☐ hard candies
- ☐ _____
- ☐ _____
- ☐ _____

**Grocery**

- [ ] rice
    - ___ white
    - ___ brown
    - ___ instant
    - ___ wild
    - ___ _____

- [ ] spaghetti/macaroni
- [ ] flour
- [ ] coffee
    - ___ percolator
    - ___ instant
    - ___ espresso
    - ___ decaffeinated
    - ___ _____

- [ ] tea
    - ___ bag
    - ___ leaf

- [ ] cocoa
- [ ] powdered milk
- [ ] oil
    - ___ olive
    - ___ vegetable
    - ___ _____

- [ ] shortening
    - ___ vegetable
    - ___ lard

- [ ] cereal
    - ___ hot
    - ___ cold
    - ___ _____
    - ___ _____

- [ ] wheat germ
- [ ] molasses
- [ ] peanut butter
- [ ] honey
- [ ] jams/jellies
    - ___ _____

- ___ _____
- ___ _____
- ___ _____

- [ ] sugar
    - ___ white
    - ___ brown
    - ___ confectioners
    - ___ _____

- [ ] baking powder/soda
- [ ] cornstarch/arrowroot
- [ ] cornmeal
- [ ] mixes
    - ___ cake
    - ___ muffins
    - ___ biscuits
    - ___ pie crust
    - ___ _____

- [ ] frostings/decorations
- [ ] baking chocolate/chips
- [ ] coconut flakes
- [ ] nuts
    - ___ pecans
    - ___ walnuts
    - ___ _____

- [ ] flavoring extracts
    - ___ vanilla
    - ___ almond
    - ___ _____

- [ ] canned pie fillings
- [ ] pudding mix/custard
- [ ] gelatin mixes
    - ___ orange
    - ___ _____

- [ ] pancake mix
- [ ] maple syrup

- [ ] ice cream toppings
- [ ] applesauce
- [ ] dried fruits
    - ___ prunes
    - ___ raisins
    - ___ _____

- [ ] canned fruits
    - ___ pineapple
    - ___ pears
    - ___ peaches
    - ___ _____
    - ___ _____

- [ ] canned juices
    - ___ apple
    - ___ cranberry
    - ___ _____
    - ___ _____
    - ___ _____

- [ ] canned vegetables
    - ___ corn
    - ___ peas
    - ___ beets
    - ___ mushrooms
    - ___ tomatoes
    - ___ yams
    - ___ _____
    - ___ _____

- [ ] canned fish
    - ___ salmon
    - ___ tuna
    - ___ sardines
    - ___ clams

- ___ crabmeat
- ___ _____

- [ ] canned luncheon meats
- [ ] spaghetti sauces
- [ ] tomato paste/sauce/puree
- [ ] canned ravioli/noodles
- [ ] canned beans
    - ___ baked
    - ___ pinto
    - ___ lentil
    - ___ _____

- [ ] canned soups
    - ___ pea
    - ___ tomato
    - ___ chicken
    - ___ chowder
    - ___ _____

- [ ] soup mixes/bouillon cubes
    - ___ _____

- [ ] dried beans/barley
    - ___ navy
    - ___ lima
    - ___ _____
    - ___ _____

- [ ] croutons
- [ ] bread crumbs
- [ ] salad dressing
- [ ] vinegar
- [ ] ketchup
- [ ] mayonnaise
- [ ] mustard
- [ ] steak sauce

- ☐ Tabasco sauce
- ☐ soy sauce
- ☐ olives/pimentos/capers
- ☐ marinated mushrooms
- ☐ pickles/relishes
- ☐ _____
- ☐ _____
- ☐ _____
- ☐ _____
- ☐ dried herbs
  - ___ basil
  - ___ oregano
  - ___ parsley
  - ___ sage
  - ___ _____
  - ___ _____
  - ___ _____
- ☐ spices
  - ___ cinnamon
  - ___ cloves
  - ___ curry
  - ___ pepper
  - ___ salt
  - ___ paprika
  - ___ minced onion
  - ___ _____
  - ___ _____
  - ___ _____
  - ___ _____
- ☐ soda
  - ___ cola
  - ___ club
  - ___ tonic
  - ___ _____
  - ___ _____
  - ___ _____

- ☐ mineral water
- ☐ beer/ale
- ☐ wine
- ☐ ethnic foods
  - ___ tacos
  - ___ Chinese noodles
  - ___ _____
  - ___ _____
- ☐ dietetic food
  - ___ _____
  - ___ _____
  - ___ _____
- ☐ baby food
  - ___ _____
  - ___ _____
- ☐ pet foods
  - ___ _____
  - ___ _____
- ☐ _____
- ☐ _____
- ☐ _____

## Meats and Fish

- ☐ beef
  - ___ steaks
  - ___ _____
  - ___ _____
  - ___ roast beef
  - ___ _____
  - ___ _____
  - ___ brisket
  - ___ chopped meat
  - ___ stew/neck bones
  - ___ liver

- ___ _____
- ___ _____
- ___ _____
- ☐ veal
  - ___ roast
  - ___ breast
  - ___ liver
  - ___ chops
  - ___ scallopini
  - ___ _____
  - ___ _____
- ☐ lamb
  - ___ leg
  - ___ chops
  - ___ stew
  - ___ _____
  - ___ _____
  - ___ _____
- ☐ pork
  - ___ roast
  - ___ shoulder
  - ___ chops
  - ___ bacon
  - ___ ham
  - ___ spareribs
  - ___ sausage
  - ___ _____
  - ___ _____
- ☐ poultry
  - ___ chicken
  - ___ turkey
  - ___ duck
  - ___ Rock Cornish hen
  - ___ _____
- ☐ frankfurters
- ☐ luncheon meats
  - ___ bologna

- ___ _____
- ___ _____
- ☐ seafood
  - ___ shrimp
  - ___ clams
  - ___ _____
  - ___ _____
- ☐ fish
  - ___ red snapper
  - ___ striped bass
  - ___ mackerel
  - ___ bluefish
  - ___ flounder
  - ___ trout
  - ___ salmon
  - ___ halibut
  - ___ filet of sole
  - ___ _____
  - ___ _____
  - ___ _____
- ☐ _____
- ☐ _____
- ☐ _____
- ☐ _____

## Checkout Counter

- ☐ chewing gum
- ☐ breath mints
- ☐ cigarettes/matches
- ☐ magazines
- ☐ newspapers
- ☐ _____
- ☐ _____
- ☐ _____
- ☐ _____

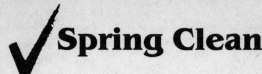 # Spring Cleaning Checklist

- Have you cut down on clutter?
- Have you reorganized to suit function?
- Have you repaired, cleaned and freshened up throughout?

## Closets

☐ Give or throw away unused shoes and clothing

☐ Clean and pack away winter clothes

☐ Look over spring and summer clothes for fit, length, pressing/cleaning

☐ Get sandals, sneakers, and other seasonal shoes in shape

☐ Wipe down shelves

☐ Line with fresh paper or paint

☐ Clear floor and clean thoroughly

☐ Review use of space. Do you need:

___ more access to frequently used items
___ regrouping of items by category
___ more shelves
___ additional rods, hooks, light
___ organizers

☐ _____

☐ _____

## Windows

☐ Remove curtains/draperies/blinds

☐ Clean (including hardware), put back up, store or switch to summer window treatment

☐ Clean screens

☐ Wash windows

## Walls

☐ Take down pictures and other removable decorations

☐ Clean/wash down walls (including woodwork, coves, and wall brackets)

☐ Clean wall decorations and replace or make changes in arrangement

☐ Repair/wallpaper/paint

☐ _____

☐ _____

## Floors

☐ Remove winter area rugs; clean and store if desired

☐ Shampoo wall-to-wall carpeting

☐ Refinish/clean and polish wood/tile floors

☐ _____

☐ _____

## Lighting

☐ Clean chandeliers and other light fixtures

☐ Clean lampshades

☐ Polish/wipe down lamps/bulbs

☐ Repair/replace cords

☐ _____

☐ _____

## Bedding

- ☐ Vacuum/clean mattress and springs
- ☐ Turn mattress around and over
- ☐ Clean and store winter blankets; replace with lightweight covers
- ☐ Remove dust ruffles and clean
- ☐ Polish/clean headboards, footboards, platforms
- ☐ _____

## Furniture, Upholstered

- ☐ Examine upholstery for tears; repair
- ☐ See if pillows need restuffing
- ☐ Vacuum/shampoo fabric
- ☐ Turn pieces over and clean
- ☐ Put on clean slipcovers if you use them
- ☐ _____
- ☐ _____

## Wood, Metal, Lucite, Formica

- ☐ Remove all objects from surface; touch up scars
- ☐ Clean surfaces and rub in long-lasting oil and polishes
- ☐ _____

## Cabinets/Shelves

- ☐ Eliminate unused items from shelves and drawers throughout home; clean or repair clocks, radios and other small appliances
- ☐ Clean out medicine chest
- ☐ Remove pots and dishes from kitchen cupboards; wipe down shelves; repaper and reorganize if needed
- ☐ Remove books, records, cassettes; dust and wipe down storage units
- ☐ Dust/polish bric-a-brac
- ☐ _____
- ☐ _____

## Attic/Basement/Porch

- ☐ Clean/vacuum/repaint walls/floors
- ☐ Give or throw away unused or unwanted items
- ☐ Dust remaining pieces
- ☐ Arrange safe storage of winter things
- ☐ Clean/refurbish porch/lawn furniture and play equipment
- ☐ Clean barbecue/outdoor grill
- ☐ _____
- ☐ _____

# ✓ Checklist for Holding a Tag Sale

- Consider holding tag sale after spring cleaning or before you move. Rummage through attic, basement, garage, closets, cupboards to see if you have enough merchandise; decide if it would be better to team up with neighbor(s) or relative(s) for larger sale.

- Allow at least three weeks to get ready. Set a weekend date that doesn't conflict with a holiday or special local event. If sale is to be held outdoors, include a rain date.

- Visit other garage sales to get an idea of the merchandise that sells well and the going price on items.

- Plan how you will advertise:

    ___ posters (make and distribute)
    ___ community bulletin boards (post handbills)
    ___ classified ads (check rates/deadlines)
    ___ public spot announcements (contact radio stations)

- Find out from local authorities if your town requires permits or has any restrictions on what you can sell or signs you can display.

- Plan how you will keep driveway clean, where customers will park and load. Tell neighbors there will be an influx of cars on that day.

- Use sheltered space such as garage for sale. Organize display area so customers have room to examine merchandise. If necessary, work out system for more lighting. Get additional folding tables and clothes rack; improvise with planks and poles. In nice weather you may want to display some merchandise outdoors.

- Set up items by categories; separate good items. (Don't overlook such collector's items as comics, baseball cards, silver, old jewelry, bottles, glassware.)

- Decide what items to spruce up or sell as-is. (Sometimes cleaning and polishing increases potential profits.) Check if electrical appliances work; label those that don't if you do no repairs. Allow time for airing out items stored in attics or basements.

- Set up white-elephant table for bargain odds and ends; put appliance table near an outlet so customers may check before buying.

- Line up extra selling help; start collecting newspapers/paper bags/shopping bags for sold items.

- Tag each item with self-adhesive labels; clearly mark the price and I.D. number, size, when applicable. Keep prices on low side to move merchandise quickly.

- Make a master list of all merchandise; include asking price, tag number, and space to note at what price item was sold.

- At least two days before sale, run newspaper/radio ads. Make sure corrected copy includes description of major sellers and/or unusual items; include your address, clear directions and day(s)/hours of sale.

- Have a large supply of small change and dollar bills.

- Day of Sale:

    ___ Put up directions and arrows to location along neighborhood routes. Take down immediately when sale is over.
    ___ Post a notice if all sales are final and you will accept only cash.
    ___ Assign specific tasks to sales help.
    ___ Have one person in charge of cash and recording sales on master list.
    ___ Be prepared to bargain, especially if sale runs a second day.

# ✔ The Well-Stocked-Bar List

## Spirits

- ☐ Scotch
- ☐ bourbon
- ☐ Canadian whisky
- ☐ vodka
- ☐ gin
- ☐ tequila
- ☐ rum (light/dark)
- ☐ _____
- ☐ _____
- ☐ brandies/cordials
  - ___ crème de menthe
  - ___ crème de cacao
  - ___ fruit brandy
  - ___ cognac
  - ___ anise liqueur
  - ___ fruit liqueur
  - ___ _____
  - ___ _____

## Wine

- ☐ apéritifs/cocktails
  - ___ sherry (dry/cream)
  - ___ vermouth (dry/sweet)
  - ___ _____
  - ___ _____
- ☐ table wines
  - ___ dry white
  - ___ _____
  - ___ _____
  - ___ fruity white
  - ___ _____

- ___ dry red
- ___ _____
- ___ _____
- ___ sweet red
- ___ _____
- ___ rosé
- ___ champagne

- ☐ dessert wines
  - ___ port
  - ___ sherry
  - ___ _____

- ☐ _____

## Beer

- ☐ light
- ☐ dark

## Fixings

- ☐ juices
  - ___ pineapple
  - ___ tomato
  - ___ lime
  - ___ _____
  - ___ _____
  - ___ _____
- ☐ citrus peels
- ☐ bitters
- ☐ grenadine
- ☐ seasonings
  - ___ salt
  - ___ pepper
  - ___ nutmeg
  - ___ mint
  - ___ _____

- ☐ olives
- ☐ pickled onions
- ☐ maraschino cherries
- ☐ fresh fruit
  - ___ _____
  - ___ _____
  - ___ _____
- ☐ sugar
- ☐ ice
  - ___ cubes
  - ___ cracked
  - ___ shavings
- ☐ water
- ☐ cream/milk
- ☐ mixers
  - ___ tonic
  - ___ club soda
  - ___ gingerale
  - ___ cola
  - ___ _____
  - ___ _____
- ☐ powdered cocktail mixes
- ☐ premixed eggnog
- ☐ _____
- ☐ _____
- ☐ _____

## Accessories

- ☐ blender
- ☐ funnel
- ☐ stirrers
- ☐ mixing spoon
- ☐ cocktail shaker
- ☐ strainer
- ☐ pitchers
  - ___ martini
  - ___ water
  - ___ _____

- ☐ ice crusher
- ☐ ice bucket/tongs
- ☐ jigger
- ☐ citrus squeezer
- ☐ corkscrew
- ☐ cork stoppers
- ☐ wine cooler/cradle
- ☐ can opener/bottle opener
- ☐ toothpicks
- ☐ cocktail napkins
- ☐ coasters
- ☐ decanters
- ☐ punch bowl/cups/server
- ☐ cocktail-mixing book
- ☐ bar cart
- ☐ glassware
  - ___ old-fashioned
  - ___ highball
  - ___ collins
  - ___ cocktail
  - ___ pony
  - ___ wine
  - ___ champagne
  - ___ brandy snifters
  - ___ cordial
  - ___ beer mugs
  - ___ pilsner
  - ___ hot-toddy mugs
  - ___ _____
  - ___ _____
- ☐ _____
- ☐ _____
- ☐ _____

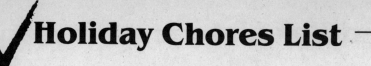

# ✔ Holiday Chores List

### Take Care of Gifts/Greetings

☐ Make holiday gift list and make and/or buy presents; save receipts for possible returns. See "Gift Idea List" and "Gift-Givers Holiday Checklist" (both in Chapter 10).

☐ Get special holiday envelopes for gift money. (Don't forget to sign your name.)

☐ Buy small Chanukah gifts and/or Christmas stocking stuffers; keep in mind unexpected young visitors.

☐ Buy wrapping paper, bows, tape, gift tags, and note cards; wrap and tag presents.

☐ Check post office deadlines to make sure gifts arrive on time; check both domestic and overseas time schedule if necessary. Wrap packages for mailing, following postal rules and regulations. Insure them if desired.

☐ Buy holiday greeting cards, stamps; update mailing list.

☐ _____

### Make Holiday Plans

☐ Call or send out party invitations; plan basic menu; arrange for extra kitchen help if needed.

☐ Make reservations for holiday trip as far in advance as possible.

☐ Get tickets for special holiday performances.

☐ Line up extra baby-sitting/child care. (Remember New Year's Eve.)

☐ Look over holiday clothing to see what you need to buy, repair, clean.

☐ Take jewelry out of safe-deposit box for holiday wear.

☐ Set up plane/train/entertainment schedules

for houseguests and visiting relatives; make arrangements for a smooth visit.

☐ Mark all plans on personal calendar; coordinate with regular schedule and school calendar.

☐ _____

☐ _____

### Prepare Home for Holidays

☐ Clean and polish up home for drop-in visitors and/or houseguests; get extra cleaning help if necessary.

☐ Do food marketing; purchase food for party; buy special foods for houseguests and extra quantities for drop-in visitors.

☐ Buy extra amounts of house staples such as paper towels, bath tissue, soap, waxed paper, foil.

☐ Buy liquor and drink fixings for holiday season drinks.

☐ Buy party supplies and snacks, hats, noisemakers.

☐ Purchase tree, accessories (wreaths). Get out ornaments and lights; trim tree. Decorate outside of house. Polish menorah and buy candles.

☐ Bake and cook ahead for party menu/holiday guests; make holiday cookies, candy recipes.

☐ Purchase last-minute items such as fresh fruit, vegetables, cut flowers and all gifts left on list.

☐ _____

☐ _____

# ✓ Informal Party Checklist

- Arrange a buffet or barbecue; consider the number of guests and how many you can accommodate comfortably.

  ☐ Will guests sit at preset smaller tables after serving themselves . . . large trestle tables . . . anywhere they can find a seat?

  ☐ If counting on good weather for outside party, do you have a back-up plan in case of rain?

- If serving cocktails, set up bar and hors d'oeuvres away from buffet, in another room or outdoors.

- Work out an easy traffic flow.

  ☐ Will you need to rearrange furniture . . . put away knickknacks?

  ☐ Do you need a separate table for serving beverages . . . for serving coffee and cake?

  ☐ Is main table placed near outlet for use of hot plates . . . keep hot foods hot, cold foods cold?

  ☐ Is buffet table organized in an easy-to-use sequence?

  ☐ Will you be able to refill platters easily?

  ☐ Will guests clear own plates . . . will you have serving help?

- Decide which you are going to use:

  ☐ plastic-coated paper plates . . . crockery

  ☐ plastic/hot-and-cold paper cups . . . glassware and cups

  ☐ plastic forks/knives/spoons . . . flatware

  ☐ paper tablecloth/napkins . . . cloth linens

- Figure out timing for barbecue so grill will be heated.

- Plan menu so that you can get most of the cooking done before guests arrive.

  ☐ Can you prepare some of the food ahead and freeze it?

☐ Is your cookware large enough to prepare needed quantities?

☐ Have you planned your menu for easy-to-eat foods . . . bite-sized . . . no-cutting . . . sandwiches?

☐ What will you prepare just before the guests arrive . . . fill wine glasses . . . butter breads?

- Check if you have everything you need for party or if you will have to borrow or rent items.

## For Barbecue

____ barbecue grill/hibachi
____ spit/hood attachment
____ electric igniter/fluid
____ charcoal briquettes/wood
____ paper/matches
____ barbecue fork/spatula/tongs
____ saucepan/long-handled basting brush
____ kebab skewers
____ water bottle (for dousing fire)/fire extinguisher
____ pot holders/oven mitt
____ meat/grill thermometer
____ cutting board
____ paring knife/carving set
____ paper towels/tinfoil
____ sponge
____ outdoor trash pail

## For Buffet

| | |
|---|---|
| ____ extra tables/chairs | ____ serving platters |
| ____ steam table/hot plate | ____ casserole dishes |
| ____ chafing dishes | ____ bread basket |
| ____ ice/ice chips | ____ salad/fruit bowl |
| ____ pitchers | ____ tablecloth/napkins |
| ____ cups/glasses | ____ plates/flatware |
| ____ coffee urn | ____ condiments |
| ____ ash trays | |

# Things to Do Before, During and After a Paint Job

## Before

☐ Set paint date well in advance; have repairs affecting paint job completed; find out how long paint job will take; arrange schedule to be home during painting so you can prepare and clean up in stages. Plan to eat out.

☐ Find out what is included in landlord's or private contractor's paint job:

‗‗‗ quality/number of coats/choice of colors/ amount of paint needed/who supplies it
‗‗‗ surface preparation/spackling/plastering
‗‗‗ ceilings/closet interiors/built-ins
‗‗‗ removing and putting back of ceiling and wall fixtures
‗‗‗ removing and putting back of doorknobs/switch plates
‗‗‗ moving and protecting furniture/carpeting/baseboards/floors/trims

☐ Check color chips available from paint store; make sure that store has all the type and color paint you need (same batch numbers) and can deliver it on schedule.

☐ Take note of all wall arrangements for return of pictures, clocks, other wall hangings. Remove objects and indicate holes to be spackled; buy and put in plastic electric outlet protectors.

☐ Bring in cartons; keep items you need daily in separate one(s); clearly label contents on each carton:

‗‗‗ blinds/shades/curtains/draperies
‗‗‗ books/wall decorations
‗‗‗ breakables/lamps/plants
‗‗‗ bathroom items in medicine chest/shower curtains

‗‗‗ closet contents
‗‗‗ kitchen counter-top items/small appliances
‗‗‗ area rugs

☐ Wipe down and clean surfaces to be painted such as cabinets, inside of medicine chest, closets, shelves.

## During and After

☐ Discuss day's work with painter each morning; doublecheck that dropcloths fully cover areas you want protected.

☐ Provide coffee/other beverages and transistor radio.

☐ Each evening prepare next day's work area and check previous day's work:

‗‗‗ sweep away loose plaster dust
‗‗‗ check paint spills/drips on furniture/floors/carpet/windows; clean immediately

☐ Hang sheets/makeshift curtains for privacy if necessary.

☐ Ask painter how long before paint is dry (takes longer on damp days); return dusted/cleaned items to original places.

☐ Have painter leave matching paint for touchups; find out the best way to clean painted surfaces and how soon you can do so.

☐ Replace wall plates/switches/doorbells/ceiling fixtures; make sure they are in good working order.

☐ Make necessary touch-ups before paint discolors.

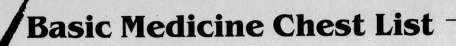 # Basic Medicine Chest List

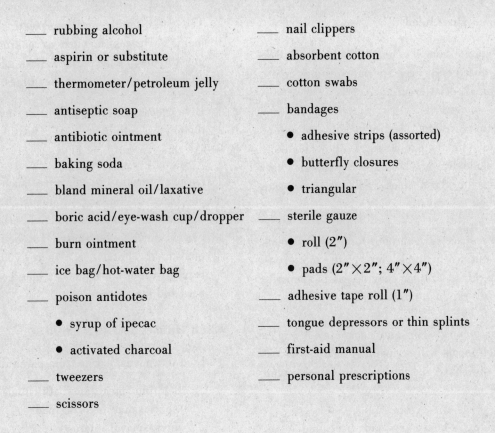

___ rubbing alcohol

___ aspirin or substitute

___ thermometer/petroleum jelly

___ antiseptic soap

___ antibiotic ointment

___ baking soda

___ bland mineral oil/laxative

___ boric acid/eye-wash cup/dropper

___ burn ointment

___ ice bag/hot-water bag

___ poison antidotes

    • syrup of ipecac

    • activated charcoal

___ tweezers

___ scissors

___ nail clippers

___ absorbent cotton

___ cotton swabs

___ bandages

    • adhesive strips (assorted)

    • butterfly closures

    • triangular

___ sterile gauze

    • roll (2″)

    • pads (2″ × 2″; 4″ × 4″)

___ adhesive tape roll (1″)

___ tongue depressors or thin splints

___ first-aid manual

___ personal prescriptions

# ✓ List to Get Ready for a Houseguest

- Do you know the purpose of visit . . . length of stay?

## Things to Do Ahead

☐ Let guest know if s/he will be sharing sleeping quarters or need special clothing for pre-planned social events.

☐ Clean/rearrange bedroom if necessary. Change linens, put out extra pillow, blankets; set aside drawer/closet space, hangers; check room for alarm clock/radio/tissues, wastebasket, ashtray.

☐ Make space in bathroom for personal items; lay out fresh towels, washcloth, toothpaste, soap, glass; arrange easy access to shampoo, shower cap, aspirin, antacid.

☐ Plan menus, shop and cook ahead. Figure which meals will be together at home or eating out; have special food and snacks available.

☐ Have extra house key made if desired.

☐ Check insurance if guest drives your car.

☐ Purchase tickets, make reservations if planning special entertainment.

☐ Prepare children for company.

☐ Check arrival time; arrange to meet houseguest.

## Things to Do on Arrival

☐ Coordinate guest and family plans . . . time together . . . time alone . . . working . . . entertaining.

☐ Arrange transportation needs . . . use of car.

- Is guest aware of your working hours . . . your children . . . your lifestyle?

☐ Tell guest family mealtimes/eating arrangements . . . access to kitchen/cooking . . . add guest items to market list . . . ask guest to tell you when s/he will miss mealtimes.

☐ Give necessary instruction on using telephone . . . appliances . . . heating/cooling systems . . . car.

☐ Go over certain circumstances such as water shortage . . . locking up home . . . how to handle telephone calls . . . if specified expenses need to be shared . . . helping with household chores . . . where you can be reached when not home . . . emergency numbers and instructions.

## When Houseguest Is a Child

☐ Find out needs/habits from parent:

____ bedtime/mealtime/bath rituals
____ special diet/favorite foods
____ toys/special interests
____ _____
____ _____

☐ Set ground rules:

____ access to refrigerator/snacking
____ use of telephone/TV/other equipment
____ bedtime
____ distance/location limits
____ knowing whereabouts
____ chores
____ _____
____ _____

☐ Set up play area:

____ stock a few toys/games
____ _____
____ _____

# ✓ Things to Remember When You Redecorate

☐ Before you start, make a list of what you want to keep or eliminate, adapt or replace.

☐ Note the specific changes you want to make; have a clear picture of how you want room(s) to look when finished; think in terms of overall effect. Keep in mind:

    ____ major function of room
    ____ mood/effect
    ____ center of interest
    ____ traffic pattern
    ____ conversation areas
    ____ activity areas
    ____ dark or light area

☐ Before making major purchases, consider the use of old pieces through rearranging, refinishing, reupholstering, or adapting for another room, another purpose.

☐ Figure out how much money and time you have to spend on this project, and what type(s) of professional help you may want to keep within these limits:

    ____ interior designer
    ____ carpenter
    ____ painter/wallpaper hanger
    ____ floor finishers/rug installers
    ____ _____

    ____ _____

☐ Plan room(s) to scale on graph paper; buy paper patterns (templates) of furniture so you can try out different arrangements on paper and see how balance works.

☐ Measure carefully; record length/width/height in notebook where you also keep receipts, swatches, etc. in one place. Don't forget to include exact measurements for:

    ____ walls/floor/ceiling
    ____ doors/doorways
    ____ windows/sills
    ____ furniture
    ____ elevator
    ____ turning area of stairwell(s)

☐ Note architectural features (jutting beams/columns, arches, composition of floor/walls); check location of all permanent features that can affect redecorating plans:

    ____ directions windows face
    ____ doors and windows in room
    ____ built-ins (shelves, closets)
    ____ electrical outlets (telephone, TV, ceiling fixtures)
    ____ cooling/heating unit(s)
    ____ _____

    ____ _____

☐ When going to stores, take along:

    ____ metal tape measure
    ____ notebook for figuring needed amounts of paint/fabric/recording estimates
    ____ fabric swatches and color paint chips

☐ Get firm answers on store and/or professional policies. Comparison shop and keep written records of all estimates and prices. Find out what specifics are included in purchases and/or contracts:

    ____ sales tax
    ____ delivery charges/date
    ____ installation fee
    ____ procedure on damaged merchandise
    ____ refund or exchange policy on unsatisfactory work or items
    ____ time period covered by warranties/guarantees
    ____ extras
    ____ _____

    ____ _____

## Don't Forget

• Redecorate to suit lifestyle (easy maintenance, entertaining, etc.).

• Allocate enough money for accessories; costs mount up quickly.

• Get samples of wallpaper/fabrics/rugs to examine at home under artificial and natural light.

• Avoid buying a piece you can't resist and then trying to make a room fit it.

• Try to redecorate one room at a time.

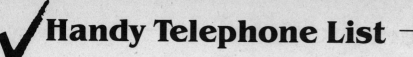

# Handy Telephone List

### Personal Routine

☐ _____ newspaper service
☐ _____ drugstore
☐ _____ liquor store
☐ _____ cleaners
☐ _____ bakery
☐ _____ florist
☐ _____ department store
☐ _____ supermarket
☐ _____ deli/grocery
☐ _____ diaper service
☐ _____
☐ _____ ticket charge-it
☐ _____ barber/beauty shop

☐ _____ gym/spa
☐ _____ local movie
☐ _____ tennis/golf club
☐ _____ library
☐ _____ adult ed
☐ _____ local Y
☐ _____
☐ _____ neighbors
☐ _____
☐ _____ friends
☐ _____
☐ _____
☐ _____ relatives
☐ _____ minister/rabbi/priest

### Business Routine

☐ _____ accountant
☐ _____ lawyer
☐ _____ insurance agent
☐ _____ stockbroker
☐ _____ bank manager
☐ _____ credit-card agencies
☐ _____
☐ _____

☐ _____ business associations
☐ _____
☐ _____ telephone-answering service
☐ _____ boss
☐ _____ secretary/assistant
☐ _____
☐ _____
☐ _____ post office

### Transportation

☐ _____ car pool
☐ _____
☐ _____ AAA
☐ _____ garage mechanic
☐ _____ parking garage

☐ _____ train/bus station
☐ _____ airline
☐ _____ taxi
☐ _____ car rental

## Children

- ☐ _____school office
- ☐ _____PTA
- ☐ _____teacher
- ☐ _____day care
- ☐ _____after-school program
- ☐ _____Scout leader
- ☐ _____Little League coach
- ☐ _____music teacher
- ☐ _____dance class
- ☐ _____karate teacher
- ☐ _____baby-sitter

- ☐ _____
- ☐ _____
- ☐ _____
- ☐ _____roller rink
- ☐ _____bowling alley
- ☐ _____pizza parlor
- ☐ _____children's friends
- ☐ _____
- ☐ _____
- ☐ _____

## Home Maintenance/Repair

- ☐ _____television
- ☐ _____heating/cooling
- ☐ _____gas
- ☐ _____electric
- ☐ _____major appliances
  - _____refrigerator/freezer
  - _____oven/range
  - _____washer/dryer
  - _____
- ☐ _____telephone

- ☐ _____handyman/super
- ☐ _____landlord/rental agent
- ☐ _____exterminator
- ☐ _____house/window cleaners
- ☐ _____snow/trash removers
- ☐ _____plumber
- ☐ _____electrician
- ☐ _____
- ☐ _____

## Medical

- ☐ _____doctor
- ☐ _____pediatrician
- ☐ _____dentist
- ☐ _____orthodontist

- ☐ _____eye doctor
- ☐ _____convalescent/nursing home
- ☐ _____veterinarian
- ☐ _____

# ✔ Emergency Telephone List

☐ _____police/local precinct

☐ _____fire

☐ _____hospital/clinic

_____

☐ _____ambulance service

☐ _____all-night taxi

☐ _____poison control

☐ _____all-night pharmacy

☐ _____all-night locksmith

☐ _____AAA road service

☐ _____utility repairs

☐ _____vet/ASPCA

☐ _____doctor's home

_____doctor's office

☐ _____nearest relative, home

_____nearest relative, office

☐ _____insurance agent, home

_____insurance agent, office

☐ _____lawyer's home

_____lawyer's office

☐ _____nearest neighbor/friend

_____

☐ _____

☐ _____

## Crisis Hotlines

☐ _____crime victim

☐ _____child abuse

☐ _____rape victim

☐ _____drug abuse

☐ _____Alcoholics Anonymous

☐ _____battered wives

☐ _____suicide prevention

☐ _____

# Your Car

☐ **New-Car Buyer's Checklist**

☐ **Gas and Mileage Checklist**

☐ **Car Insurance Checklist**

☐ **Things to Remember for a Car Accident/Claim**

☐ **Car Security Checklist**

☐ **Used-Car Buyer's Checklist**

☐ **Car Maintenance and Tune-up Checklist**

☐ **Car Emergency Items List**

# New-Car Buyer's Checklist

### Shopping

☐ Know how much money you wish to spend and what accessories or extras you think are important to buy. (Keep in mind you may not be replacing this car for five to ten years.) Find out what items are standard equipment in some cars and are extra in others:

____ automatic transmission

____ power steering/power brakes

____ air conditioning

____ back-up lights/fog lights/four-way emergency flashers

____ AM/FM stereo/tape deck/CB/sideband radio

____ tinted windows/window washers

____ electric windows/locks/digital clock

____ electrically controlled seat position

____ white-walled tires/deluxe wheel covers

____ burglar alarm

____ _____

____ _____

____ _____

☐ Shop around; look at consumer/auto magazines and federal requirement standards posted at all dealer showrooms. Compare safety records, durability, gas and mileage performance ratings, insurance costs.

☐ Check out dealer and service department:

____ location convenient to your home/business

____ hours open

____ dependable reputation/responsive to customer needs

____ preferred customer treatment

____ complaints registered with Better Business Bureau

☐ Check car for size and comfort of your family. Look at legroom, headroom; if seats move forward and back enough. See if there is enough trunk space. Note any special features/limitations such as space-saving spare tire.

☐ Road-test the model you are considering. See how well it meets your needs:

____ for visibility

____ on start-ups

____ using the passing gear

____ up hills

____ cornering

____ smooth riding

## Ordering

☐ Doublecheck that the order/bill of sale your salesperson writes up includes all the optional equipment clearly written out with the cost. Find out what is included at no extra cost to you. Don't sign the order until you are satisfied that it covers:

    ___ color (outside/inside), style/number of doors

    ___ interior accessories/fabrics

    ___ tires (spare), seatbelts (note length)

    ___ dealer preparation (it is illegal to charge for this in many states)

    ___ undercoating/body-coat protection

☐ Check your warranty carefully (it is usually a combination of a limited and full warranty). Make sure you understand the terms (especially those which may void your guarantee):

    ___ what defective parts are fixed/replaced free of charge/no labor charge or with labor charge

    ___ what parts are not covered

    ___ credit based on how long you used product

    ___ if parts can't be fixed after a number of tries, you get a choice of new ones or your money back

    ___ owner doesn't have to do anything unreasonable (ship car to factory)

    ___ car emergency repairs done by authorized dealer away from home

    ___ months or mileage warranty (whichever comes first)

    ___ prescribed car tune-up schedule

    ___ using only certain recommended products or parts

## Before Taking Ownership

☐ Check that your bill of sale matches the equipment and services listed on the car sticker (factory equipment) and those listed on your order that dealer installs. Federal law requires that the sticker remain on the car window until delivery to customer. Insist that discrepancies be corrected immediately.

☐ Keep matching bill of sale and sticker for your records.

☐ Examine car for imperfections; have it serviced by the dealer, including dealer preparation; have all adjustments made, or get in writing, before you take the car home, that these will be done at no charge.

☐ Take the car out for a road test, if possible. Check that odometer and brakes work properly; listen for squeaks and rattles. (Rattles and water leak guarantee runs out in ninety days.) Have adjustments made; have dealer put them in writing.

☐ Get all necessary transfer papers and disclosure statements from the dealer:

    ___ odometer reading at time of transfer/date of transfer

    ___ seller's name/address/signature

    ___ make/body type/year/model/vehicle identification number

    ___ title registration (if your state requires it)

    ___ statement certifying that seller complied with Motor Vehicle Information and Cost Savings Act

# ✓ Gas and Mileage Checklist

Do you get the most mileage for your gas?

**Examine Your Driving Habits**

Do you
___ drive at steady/moderate speeds (between 30–55 m.p.h.)
___ accelerate slowly
___ brake as little as possible
___ build momentum as you climb a hill/take advantage of gravity when going downhill
___ avoid idling car engine for more than one minute
___ turn ignition off when waiting on lines
___ place transmission in neutral when you stop in traffic
___ carry minimum weight in trunk/on roof
___ arrange smaller pieces of luggage on front of car rack to minimize wind resistance
___ limit use of the air conditioner
___ avoid spillage by not overfilling tank/buy gas when gauge shows a quarter tank or less
___ combine errands for fewer trips/avoid frequent stops/use car pools

**Look at the Condition of Your Car**

☐ Are the tires properly inflated? Is tire pressure raised to the maximum? Do you check it at least once a month?

☐ Are your wheels properly aligned?

☐ Are your brakes adjusted so they do not drag?

☐ Are your spark plugs clean and firing properly?

☐ Are your oil and air filters clean?

☐ Have you considered buying radial tires?

☐ Do you get a tune-up for your car according to the manufacturer's recommended time schedule?

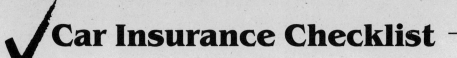

# Car Insurance Checklist

- Examine your car insurance to see exactly who is covered, under what conditions and for what amounts; evaluate if you have the basic types of coverage that you need.

☐ How well protected are you in case of a liability suit for bodily injury and/or property damage?

    ___ What is the limit the company will pay to any one person in any one accident?

    ___ What is the maximum amount paid for all injuries occurring in one accident?

    ___ Are you aware that if a court awarded higher damages than the maximum stated in your policy, you would have to pay the difference?

☐ Are you covered in case of an accident involving a hit-and-run driver, an uninsured motorist or one whose insurance company has become insolvent?

☐ Are medical payments made immediately (to you/your family/passengers) without determining who is at fault? Do services include:

    ___ medical
    ___ surgical
    ___ X ray
    ___ dental
    ___ prosthetic devices
    ___ ambulance
    ___ hospital care
    ___ professional nursing
    ___ funeral expenses

☐ Do you need comprehensive physical damage coverage?

☐ Is the value of your car too low to justify having collision insurance?

☐ Does your state have a no-fault insurance law? If so, how do its requirements affect your coverage as far as:

    ___ when a person has the right to sue
    ___ inclusion/exclusion of property damage
    ___ amounts paid to persons who lose income
    ___ amounts paid for medical expenses
    ___ amount paid to people performing essential services for those injured

- Investigate your options after reviewing your needs.

  ☐ Can you raise your deductible to reduce your premiums?

  ☐ Are you taking advantage of discount possibilities?

  ___ safe driving records
  ___ multiple car ownership
  ___ economy package policy
  ___ teen driver's good grades
  ___ driver education degree
  ___ over-65 driver education class

- Contact your state Commissioner of Insurance to check out:

  ☐ any legal requirements for minimum car insurance you must carry

  ☐ on what basis to compare differing policies available

  ☐ an insurance company's reputation for handling claims and its financial solvency

# ✔ Things to Remember for a Car Accident/Claim

## On the Scene

☐ Stop, turn off ignition, don't smoke. Get vehicle(s) out of traffic, if allowed by state law; if not, warn oncoming motorists of the accident.

☐ Summon help (ambulance) for the injured. (Don't administer first aid unless you are sure it's warranted and you have the proper training.) Be wary of moving injured persons.

☐ Notify the police immediately. If you cannot think clearly at this time, say so. Answer all questions, but don't give sketchy information which may not be accurate and can work against you later.

☐ Get the investigating officer's name, badge number, jurisdiction, and the accident report number.

☐ Exchange only specific information with driver of the other vehicle. Write down:

    ____ driver's name

    ____ address

    ____ driver's license number

    ____ car registration number/license number

    ____ car make, model, year

    ____ insurance company and policy number

☐ Refuse to sign any liability waivers or assurances that you are not hurt or injured, and do not discuss the accident or your insurance coverage; do not accept responsibility or admit fault.

☐ Obtain names and addresses of all passengers; note where each passenger was seated; who was/was not injured.

☐ Scout around for any witnesses; take down their names and addresses.

☐ Refuse any legal assistance or payments at the scene of the accident.

☐ Beware of unsolicited tow trucks which appear on the scene.

☐ Record the circumstances and as many details as you can. Write down:

    ____ where accident occurred

    ____ time of day/lighting conditions

    ____ road conditions

    ____ approximate speed of vehicles

    ____ signs/signals that have a bearing on the accident

    ____ any evidence of violations of the law

☐ Diagram the accident as accurately as possible; note direction/placement of cars and people. If you have a camera, take photos of cars and surroundings. Note skid marks and any debris.

☐ Keep bills and receipts for medical attention that you or your passengers receive.

☐ Away from home, find nearest insurance office listed on the back of your policy or in the yellow pages.

## Before Making a Claim

☐ Find out your state's law on the amount of time it takes to settle a claim.

☐ Note if both vehicles in the accident are covered by the same company; your deductible amount may be waived in collision.

☐ Ask claims adjuster about collecting the cost of repairs from the other driver/insurance company. (The amount you will be refunded, including your deductible, will depend on how much your company collects, the company's procedures, and/or the state's regulations.)

☐ Check if you have exceeded your medical policy limits; find out if the other driver is protected by liability. (You may have to deal directly with the driver's insurance company if s/he is at fault.)

☐ Check state's no-fault laws if applicable; you may be able to collect medical and related expenses immediately.

# Car Security Checklist

**DON'T**

___ Leave engine running or keys in car ignition.

___ Hide spare keys in car/leave registration in glove compartment.

___ Place purse or packages beside you when driving.

___ Hitchhike or pick up hitchhikers.

___ Leave your car if it breaks down and ride with a stranger for help.

___ Tag your car keys with name/address/license number.

___ Enter parked car before walking around it to check out front- and back-seat floor.

**AVOID**

___ Driving through high-crime areas.

___ Parking on dark side streets.

**DO**

___ Roll up windows/turn on antitheft devices/lock car when you leave.

___ Carry car registration with you.

___ Keep glove compartment locked.

___ Place purse on floor and lock packages in trunk.

___ Travel well-lit streets even if it takes longer.

___ Leave only the ignition key when you park in pay lot or bring car in for servicing.

___ Turn on emergency flashers and get off road if car has trouble. In case of accident, place flares behind car to ward off traffic. Raise hood/tie handkerchief to aerial or door/get back in car and lock doors/wait for police.

___ Park under street light or in front of bright store window at night.

___ Blow horn (SOS) and go to nearest gas or police station (not home) if harassed by another car.

___ Etch your social security number on valuable car parts.

**Devices that Discourage Theft**

Check reliable auto-parts store for specific recommendations to suit your car and budget. Consider:

- ignition "kill" system with secret switch
- tapered door-lock knobs
- collar/bar to lock steering wheel and brake pedal together

- lock-type gas cap
- inside locking hood release
- alarm system/burglar alarm decal on car window

# Used-Car Buyer's Checklist

☐ Check references of car seller/dealers; get names of people who have used dealer and service department. (New-car dealers are often the best bet for used-car purchase.)

☐ Keep a critical eye open when visiting each dealer or seller. Take note of:

___ dirty car lots (usually indicate poor service record)

___ how long dealer has been at this address

___ seller/dealers who won't let you test-drive the car or inspect it

___ dealers who insist on a deposit for a test-drive (don't do it)

___ seller/dealers who only let you look at the car at night or in the rain

___ seller/dealers who refuse to let your mechanic/diagnostic center check out car

☐ Be suspicious of any unbelievably low prices. Keep in mind:

___ 12,000 miles per year on a car is average

___ the servicing record on the car is pasted on the inside hood or inside car-door frame

___ you will spend from $150 to $500 to get a used car into proper working order

___ if car is too old, its parts can only be replaced with used parts from a junkyard (manufacturers must supply parts for ten years)

___ low mileage on a used car may mean owner problems

___ low resale value of a gas-eating car

___ public vehicle (taxi, police car) must be indicated as such when resold

___ high running expenses/high cost of maintenance/repair

☐ Examine the car closely for makeshift repairs/unethical reconditioning devices to make items appear new. Look for:

___ unmatched set of tires

___ new rugs on floor that cover rusted-out parts

___ undercoating or repaint job which hides welding from major accident (it is illegal to sell unless stated in writing)

___ removal of good battery and replacing it with old one

☐ Check out the car's overall condition. Be on the lookout for:

___ compression of engine (have mechanic check front end)

___ rusted-out frame/rear fenders/doors

___ leaking brake fluid on tire sides

___ dents/ripples on car body

___ leaking transmission fluid under car

___ cracks on windows

___ car not level (weak springs or leaking shock absorbers)

___ cracked or old battery

☐ Test-drive the car and note how well it drives. See if any of the following problems appear:

___ odometer not working properly (red-purplish color/numbers uneven may indicate tampering)

___ brakes pulling (to right or left)

_____ vibrations of steering wheel

_____ unusual noises/vibrations from engine/ transmission/rear end

_____ noises/vibrations during idling

_____ musty, dank odor inside car (may indicate car has been in a flood)

_____ transmission hesitates/jerks

_____ smoke from rear exhaust

_____ low power on uphill grade

_____ car pulls to either side

☐ Don't sign the contract until you understand the financial arrangements and the warranty. Consider:

_____ sales manager/owner sit in so s/he can't play ignorant if problems arise later

_____ if warranty on car covers a second owner

_____ how long warranty is in effect; what is covered for parts and labor

_____ if dealer thinks you'll be paying cash, s/he may increase the price

_____ finance charges may include fees other than interest which may not be deducted from taxes (get breakdown from dealer)

_____ implied or inferred warranty statements can usually be taken to legal authorities

☐ Get all necessary papers from dealer/seller:

_____ mileage disclosure statement

_____ title transfer (in states where applicable)

_____ warranty papers

_____ financing agreement if necessary

# ✓ Car Maintenance and Tune-up Checklist

**Possible for Do-It-Yourselfers**

☐ Battery

   \_\_\_\_ cover metal plates with distilled water
   \_\_\_\_ clean corroded battery terminals
   \_\_\_\_ test charging capacity of battery fluid

☐ Spark plugs

   \_\_\_\_ remove and inspect to see that they are not gray or tan
   \_\_\_\_ clean and adjust electrodes to specific gap
   \_\_\_\_ replace after 10,000–15,000 miles

☐ Oil/filter

   \_\_\_\_ change oil every 2,000–3,000 miles
   \_\_\_\_ change filter at the same time
   \_\_\_\_ clean oil filler cap

☐ Distributor points/related parts

   \_\_\_\_ inspect cap for damage; replace if necessary
   \_\_\_\_ check rotor; replace if necessary
   \_\_\_\_ inspect high-tension wire; replace if necessary
   \_\_\_\_ check breaker points for burns/pitting
   \_\_\_\_ file damaged breaker points/clean/replace after 10,000–15,000 miles
   \_\_\_\_ adjust and gap points according to car specifications
   \_\_\_\_ install new condenser with new points
   \_\_\_\_ adjust timing on distributor (use timing-light tester

☐ Lubrication

   \_\_\_\_ lube high spots on distributor shaft (use high-temperature lubricant)
   \_\_\_\_ lube chassis (according to owner's manual)
   \_\_\_\_ clean/lube manifold heat-control valve

☐ Radiator

   \_\_\_\_ check for slow leaks/repair
   \_\_\_\_ check coolant levels/flush/add more if needed
   \_\_\_\_ add antifreeze in autumn

☐ Hoses/fan belts

    ___ check for signs of wear/cracks/bulging/replace if necessary

☐ Tires

    ___ check air pressure against amount stated in owner's manual
    ___ check wheel alignment
    ___ balance tires (look for excessive wear on one spot/area)

☐ Car lights

    ___ check headlights
    ___ see if brake lights are working
    ___ check taillights
    ___ make sure directional signals are working

## For a Mechanic/Garage to Check Out

☐ Cylinder

___ measure compression for each cylinder
___ check worn rings/defective valves/ruptured head gasket

☐ Electrical components

    ___ check output of alternator/generator/voltage regulator
    ___ check starter/ignition coil

☐ Carburetor/air combustion parts

    ___ remove and clean carburetor air cleaner/replace if necessary
    ___ clean and test automatic choke
    ___ replace or clean air fuel filter
    ___ set screw for dependable idling speed mixture

☐ Valves

    ___ adjust mechanical lifters for proper openings

☐ Brakes/clutch

    ___ test/tighten/replace brake shoes
    ___ check fluid levels

☐ Pollution-control systems

    ___ check/clean/replace valve for pvc system
    ___ clean filters in air pump and evaporative control canister

# ✔ Car Emergency Items List

### In the Trunk

\_\_\_\_ spare tire

\_\_\_\_ pump inflator/friction tape

\_\_\_\_ jack and lug wrench

\_\_\_\_ fire extinguisher (dry chemical)

\_\_\_\_ road flares

\_\_\_\_ spare fan belt

\_\_\_\_ battery jumper cables

\_\_\_\_ empty can/siphon hose

\_\_\_\_ plastic sheet

\_\_\_\_ tool kit including

- adjustable small wrench

- pliers

- screwdrivers

\_\_\_\_ first-aid kit*

### In the Glove Compartment

\_\_\_\_ clean rags

\_\_\_\_ spare fuses

\_\_\_\_ power beam spotlight

\_\_\_\_ pocket knife

\_\_\_\_ car owner's manual

\_\_\_\_ name/address/telephone number to call in emergency

*See First Aid Supply List for Camping, p. 28.

# Your Children

□ List to Get Ready for Your First Baby

□ Working Parents' Checklist for Child Care

□ List for Traveling with Your Baby

□ Birthday Party Checklist

□ List of Basic Gifts for Children

□ Parents' Checklist for Child's Hospital Stay

□ Parents' Checklist for Baby-Sitter

□ Checklist for Choosing a Camp

□ Getting-Kids-Ready-for-Camp List

□ Back-to-School Checklist

□ Child Security List

□ Checklist for a Teacher's Conference

□ Checklist for Choosing a College

□ Off-to-College List

# ✔ List to Get Ready for Your First Baby

## In the First Three Months

- ☐ Choose obstetrician; make note of doctor appointments, including dental checkup.

- ☐ Review health insurance policy for obstetric coverage; check hospital and doctor rates; make payment arrangements.

- ☐ Preregister for type of hospital room or birth-room setting you want. (Your doctor may have to reserve the bed.) Find out if rooming-in is an option.

- ☐ Be sure to arrange for someone (housekeeper, cleaning help, neighbor, relative) to help you during the first few weeks after baby is born. If you plan on having a baby nurse, interview several and book one early.

- ☐ Notify your employer; check company maternity benefits for leave time if you expect to be a working mother.

## During Months Four through Eight

- ☐ Check with friends and relatives about possible items you need to borrow; keep a "return" list. Borrow/buy maternity clothes.

- ☐ Start planning how you want to set up baby's room; borrow/buy nursery equipment; if painting furniture or walls, use nontoxic, lead-free paint.

  - ___ chest of drawers
  - ___ bassinet or cradle/crib
  - ___ crib mattress/waterproof pad/bumpers
  - ___ dressing table/plastic tub/bath tray
  - ___ room/bath thermometer
  - ___ lined hamper

- ___ diaper pail with tight cover (if you plan to use cloth diapers)
- ___ rocker or easy chair/footstool
- ___ small table
- ___ lamp/night light
- ___ wastebasket

- ___ _____
- ___ _____

- ☐ Sign up for prenatal and/or parenthood classes; find out if hospital offers orientation tour of labor/delivery areas.

- ☐ Plan and shop for baby's layette; ask about delivery dates. Keep in mind that babies outgrow early purchases quickly and that baby gifts (sacque sets, blanket sleeper) will arrive soon after the baby.

  - ___ fitted crib sheets (4–6)
  - ___ waterproof sheeting (1)
  - ___ quilted pads (4–6)
  - ___ crib blankets (2–3)
  - ___ outdoor blanket
  - ___ flannel receiving blankets (3–6)

  - ___ _____
  - ___ _____

  - ___ soft baby towels (3–4)
  - ___ washcloths (4–6)
  - ___ bibs (2–4)
  - ___ waterproof diaper bag
  - ___ diapers (dozen cloth even if using diaper service or disposables; four dozen otherwise)

___ diaper safety pins (dozen)

___ disposable diaper liners (package)

___ waterproof pants (2)

___ snap-knit undershirts (4–6)

___ front-opening cotton knit gowns (3–4)

___ christening gown

___ _____

___ _____

___ stretch suits (2–4)

___ lightweight sweaters (2)

___ socks/bootees (2–4)

___ pram snowsuit/snap mittens

___ hat (knitted cap/sunbonnet)

___ snap-crotch overalls (2–4)

___ snap wide-neck (long/short sleeve) shirts (2–4)

___ _____

___ _____

☐ Arrange for diaper service if you plan to use one.

☐ Choose baby names. Decide about birth announcements; make printing arrangements; make up mailing list.

☐ Choose godparents; get in touch with clergyperson/rabbi about religious ceremony.

☐ Interview and choose a pediatrician with whom you feel compatible.* Discuss method of feeding (breast or bottle), sterilizing bottles, vitamins, early bath care. Adjust supply list accordingly.

___ brushes (bottle, nipple)

*See "Checklist for Choosing a Doctor," p. 169.

___ extra nipples/collars

___ bottle covers

___ bottles (4–ounce, 8–ounce)

___ sterilizer with rack/lid

___ quart measuring cup (glass)

___ funnel/timer

___ bottle tongs

___ baby-food grinder

___ feeding dish/utensils

___ _____

___ _____

___ _____

___ baby lotion/powder

___ baby shampoo/soap

___ rubbing alcohol

___ baby thermometer/petroleum jelly

___ diaper-rash cream

___ cotton swabs

___ nose/ear syringe

___ nail scissors

___ baby brush/comb

___ covered jar for sterile water/cotton balls

___ tissues

___ pacifiers

___ vaporizer or humidifier

___ health-care paperback

___ _____

___ _____

## Ninth Month

☐ Pack suitcase. Leave valuables home, including purse. (Your husband can bring anything you need later such as your going-home outfit.)

☐ Arrange for care of pets, plants. Stock refrigerator and cupboard with easy-to-use foods, and/or precook casseroles for freezer.

☐ Arrange cleaning help.

## While in the Hospital

☐ Telephone diaper service and store about layette deliveries; notify baby nurse; make final arrangements for religious ceremony.

☐ Give printer baby's name for announcements; send out birth announcements.

☐ Order first-day photos.

☐ Inform lawyer/insurance agent to change legal documents affected by baby's birth.

### Ready-to-Go Suitcase

- washable gowns/pajamas
- robe/bed jacket/slippers
- nursing bras/pads
- shower cap
- underpants
- sanitary belt
- hairbrush/comb/pins
- toothbrush/paste
- deodorant
- perfume
- cosmetic bag
- makeup mirror
- manicure set/nail polish
- tweezer
- eyeglasses/contacts/case
- shopping bags
- roll of dimes for telephone
- book/magazines
- stationery/stamps
- pad/pen/pencil
- telephone—address book
- clock radio
- _____
- _____

### Labor Bag for Natural Childbirth

- Chapstick
- sour candies/lollipops
- stopwatch
- washcloth
- ice pack
- _____
- _____

### For Bringing Baby Home

- receiving blankets
- bunting (if winter)
- crib blanket or carriage shawl
- sweater/hat
- undershirt
- gown
- socks or bootees
- rubber pants
- newborn disposable diapers or cloth diapers
- diaper pins

### Equipment for Baby's First Year

- infant seat
- carriage
- play pen/pad
- feeding table or high chair
- stroller
- toilet seat or chair
- portable crib
- electrical outlet covers
- safety gate/latches/window bars
- _____
- _____

# ✔ Working Parents' Checklist for Child Care

☐ Is child ready to leave home environment . . . does s/he need to play with other children?

☐ Which would work best for you . . . group or individual child care?

- Locate group facilities (public and private) by calling city or state social services and checking telephone directory.

- Get individual recommendations from other mothers, housekeepers, your pediatrician; check local bulletin boards, placement office of nursing schools/college, state employment office, senior citizen centers, classifieds ads.

**Group Care (day care center or family day care, home-based)**

- Before visiting, find out:

  ☐ distance from home and office
  ☐ transportation requirements
  ☐ days and hours available/extended day/holidays
  ☐ fee and payment schedule/extra costs
  ☐ attendance policy (penalty for late pick-up)
  ☐ sponsor, if any
  ☐ training/experience of person(s) in charge
  ☐ number of children/age range/diversity
  ☐ how children are grouped

- Visit more than one center or day-care home; try to be there when parents drop off children. Note how you think your child will react to staff, children, environment.

  ☐ Is environment safe and healthy?

    ___ sufficient exits
    ___ fenced-in outdoor area
    ___ adequate ventilation and lighting
    ___ clean bathroom and kitchen
    ___ sufficient space for number of children
    ___ separate rest/sleeping area
    ___ provision for sick children
    ___ nurse/doctor on call
    ___ nutritious meals/snacks

☐ Is program/atmosphere supportive and lively?

    ___ children involved in what they are doing
    ___ pursue interests according to abilities
    ___ space and materials set up to meet children's needs
    ___ separate quiet and active play areas
    ___ place where child can be alone
    ___ materials within easy reach
    ___ children play well together

☐ Are materials sufficient and suitable?

    ___ appropriate for number/age of children
    ___ varied to include free-form (clay, sand, blocks) and structured (trains, dolls, puzzles)

☐ Are adults responsive to children?

    ___ know them individually
    ___ encourage curiosity, initiative
    ___ listen and answer questions openly
    ___ share attention and affection
    ___ children seem to like and trust person(s) in charge

☐ How are sensitive situations handled?

    ___ separations
    ___ toilet accidents
    ___ fighting among children

- Warning Signals

  - ☐ no typical daily schedule
  - ☐ children wander aimlessly or are glued to TV
  - ☐ boys and girls are expected to behave and play differently
  - ☐ keeping order is top priority; constant do's and don't's are heard
  - ☐ most children do not attend regularly
  - ☐ parent visits are not encouraged

- Interview director/person in charge; discuss your observations. Inquire about turnover of children and helpers; find out if a staff member takes care of same child on continuing basis; check insurance policy.

- Speak to other parents using facility. Ask if it's easy to set up a private meeting to discuss child. Find out what they like least and most about arrangement and if they would recommend it.

- Visit again with child.

  - ☐ Does set-up offer the flexibility you need?
  - ☐ Is this an environment that will help your child develop?
  - ☐ Would your child fit in, feel secure?
  - ☐ Would you feel comfortable leaving child here when you go to work?

**Individual Care\***

- Call job applicants and find out:

  - ☐ where person lives; distance from your home
  - ☐ flexibility of working time

\*For individual care outside your home refer to criteria in first section of this checklist.

- ☐ prior experience
- ☐ recent references
- ☐ TB test within the year

- Review what you think are the most important qualities candidate should have before calling references. Call references to check personal qualities, reliability, health, consistency of care, how long on job, why left.

- Find out if insurance covers child-care situation; see if workmen's compensation applies in your state.

- Write out job description:

  - ☐ daily child-care routines; outdoor activities, arranging visits for playmates, driving child to appointments
  - ☐ daily/weekly household chores; pet and plant care, marketing, preparing dinners
  - ☐ working days/hours; time off daily/ weekly, flexibility
  - ☐ financial arrangement; salary/review/ overtime, transportation costs, social security payments, sick leave, vacation pay, insurance
  - ☐ living-in; room/accessories, access privileges, ground rules for personal conduct

- Interview several individuals. Be clear about priorities. Make sure baby/child is present part of the time to see interaction; ask person how s/he would handle specific situations of concern to you.

- Do you agree on the basics the job covers? How good is communication between you? Is the person willing to work for short trial period?

# ✓ List for Traveling with Your Baby

☐ See pediatrician early enough about necessary shots so reaction won't interfere with trip. Discuss travel restrictions and health care. Get note from doctor to present to airline stating newborn baby can fly. Ask about diet changes (formula) related to travel.

☐ Give baby a week or so to get used to new equipment, disposable diapers, diet changes.

☐ Test out portable equipment:

    ____ portacrib/playpen
    ____ collapsible stroller
    ____ front/back carrier
    ____ reclining infant seat/belt
    ____ car restraint with harness

    ____ _____

☐ Make room reservations; check if motel/hotel has crib, access to refrigerator. Take along an immersion coil for heating water.

☐ Pack baby's things separately. Check out supplies (clothing, bedding, toiletries) in "List to Get Ready for Your First Baby," page 00.

☐ Take insulated diaper bag with:

    ____ change of clothing

____ sweater/bonnet
____ disposable diapers/liners/diaper pins
____ diaper-rash cream
____ plastic bag with moist washcloth or premoistened towelettes
____ baby towel
____ washable toy
____ security blanket
____ set of measuring spoons
____ pacifier
____ baby spoon
____ teething biscuits
____ sterilized water/spillproof container
____ extra nipples/covers
____ plastic bottles (for formula/juice)
____ baby food

____ _____
____ _____
____ _____

☐ Keep baby on accustomed feeding and nap schedule whenever possible; leave a little before naptime or travel at night. Feed baby before you eat; when you go into restaurant, bring in finger food/toy; ask for out-of-the-way table.

## By Plane

• Book flight when less crowded (off hours/early in week); you may get empty seat next to you.

• Find out what facilities/supplies are on board for babies.

• Reserve bassinet row seat (no smoking) whenever possible; if needed, reserve bassinet.

• Have tickets/boarding pass mailed to you if time permits.

• Get to airport early; notify airline personnel where you are in lounge so you and baby can board first or last.

• Hold baby in your arms with seat belt around you at take-off and landing; take extra bottle of juice or milk for use during these changes in air pressure.

• Carry on enough formula for feedings during plane trip; store in aircraft refrigerator; attendant will warm on request.

## By Car

- Make sure baby is held in place with properly secured car safety restraint (right size).

- Cover vinyl with soft towel in warm weather to keep from getting hot and sticky.

- Dress baby in easy wear-and-care clothing; shoeless in summer.

- Keep back window ledge free of loose objects.

- Make frequent stops; let baby move around outside on blanket.

- Do not reuse opened baby food unless you are carrying portable refrigerator.

- Attach a few colorful toys to restraint seat with short string; bring bag of surprise toys for older baby.

# Birthday Party Checklist

☐ Make up guest list and set date.

☐ Decide location and type of party. Have backup plan for outdoor party in case of rain.

☐ Organize party around a theme in decorations and games adapted to child's age. Standbys:

____ costume

____ treasure hunt

____ magic/puppet show

____ cartoons

____ _____

____ skating/bowling

____ disco

____ pajama party/overnight

____ _____

____ _____

☐ Reserve space if necessary; work out transportation plan. Contact person/organization to clear date, time, fees if you plan on live entertainment such as a mime or magician.

☐ Go over supply list to see what you need to buy or make.

☐ Send written invitation including date, time, place, RSVP. Note:

____ definite time to start and end

____ if serving a meal

____ if pick-up place is not your home

____ your telephone number

____ type of party in case guests need to dress a special way or bring equipment

☐ Plan party around loosely organized activity; alternate active and quiet games.

____ have adult referee any contests

____ steer clear of games that put guest on the spot

____ avoid long waits for turns

____ team or pair up young children to encourage participation

____ activities adaptable for all ages:
  • pitching pennies
  • singalongs
  • charades
  • dancing
  • balloon relays
  • hamming it up with a tape recorder

☐ Plan and fill loot bags/prize grab bag; keep out of reach until party's end. Decide ahead when gifts will be opened and be sure child understands.

☐ Ask other parent or another adult to help out on party day, or hire a teen to help.

### Day-of-Party Reminders

• Pick up birthday cake
• Place breakables out of reach
• Set party table, hang decorations, blow up balloons
• Rehearse new games with child, keeping directions simple
• Keep written party schedule for easy reference
• Assemble candles, matches; defrost ice-cream cake
• Keep camera/flash handy to take photos for family album

## Supply List

*Invitations*

stamps, addresses

*Decorations*

balloons

tablecloth

napkins

paper cups

paper plates

plastic forks/spoons

blowers/horns

hats

_____

_____

_____

*Entertainment*

record player

records

tape recorder

pennies

_____

_____

_____

_____

*Camera*

flash

film

*Candles*

holders

matches

*Loot bags and filler items*

_____

_____

_____

_____

*Prizes*

_____

_____

_____

*Refreshments*

cake

ice cream

soda/juice/milk/punch

candy

nuts/pretzels/potato chips

cake knife/platter/bowls

straws

simple meal ingredients

___ hot dogs

___ pizza

___ _____

___ _____

___ _____

# List of Basic Gifts for Children

## Infants

- crib mobile
- activity board
- crib gym
- plastic music box
- rattle
- bright cloth doll/soft ball
- knitted/rubber animals
- floating tub toy
- nonglass mirror
- _____
- _____
- carriage covers
- silver feeding spoon
- teething ring
- feeding dish/warmer
- playpen
- portacrib
- back carrier
- umbrella stroller
- toy chest
- _____
- _____

## Toddlers/ Preschoolers

- push–pull toys
- wooden pounding bench
- plastic music box
- plastic snap beads
- stacking toys
- nesting toys
- four-wheel riding toys
- wagon
- cuddly animal toys
- cloth picture books
- rubber dolls
- bubbles and pipe
- pop-up boxes
- _____
- _____
- indoor gym
- rocking toy
- Big Wheel riding toy
- balls, all sizes
- tricycle
- sled
- kindergarten blocks
- heavy truck/train/ car/movable parts
- large stringing beads
- simple wooden puzzles
- picture lotto
- large dominoes
- large magnet
- large magnifier
- play house/play people
- play airport/hospital/ school bus/telephone/dishes
- pin-up ruler
- picture books
- small record player/ records
- small rhythm set
- dress-up hats
- dolls for dressing
- cuddly hand/finger puppets
- rubber dolls
- bath soap crayons
- play dough
- easel/finger paints
- large crayons/ construction paper
- gummed colored paper/blunt scissors
- sewing boards
- roller skates
- _____
- _____

## Ages Six through Ten

- blackboard/colored chalk
- jumping rope
- hula hoop
- kite
- door gym bar
- roller skates
- ice skates
- bicycle
- bat/softball/glove
- large rubber balls
- sled
- bookbag
- subscription to children's magazine
- books
- records
- drum set
- recorder
- harmonica
- world globe
- ant farm
- pet
- walkie-talkie
- dollhouse/furniture/ toy farms/forts/castles
- reproductions of household equipment
- dolls/comic-book heroes/outfits
- stuffed animals
- wooden building blocks, varied shapes
- interlocking building sets
- electric train set

- woodworking tools/belt
- stethoscope
- disguise/makeup kit
- simple magic set
- hand puppets
- puppet theater
- simple loom
- board games
- magnetic dart game
- spinning tops
- marbles
- jacks
- pickup sticks
- jigsaw puzzles
- modeling clay
- paper cutouts
- colored marker set
- coloring books
- stamp collection hobby
- model making
- _____

- _____
- _____

### Pre-teen/Teen

- bulletin/memo board
- desk set
- calendar
- posters
- lock diary
- stationery
- scrapbook/photo album
- telephone-address book
- personalized pen/pencils
- photo wallet
- clock radio
- calculator
- camera/accessories
- cassette tape recorder
- binoculars
- bowling ball

- soccer ball
- football
- tennis racket
- baseball glove
- shoe roller skates/ice skates
- camping gear
- bicycle
- piggy banks
- bookbag
- jewelry/jewelry box
- key ring
- watch
- hairbrush/comb set
- scented soap/bubble bath
- clothing
- chess set/backgammon set
- board games
- jigsaw puzzles
- word and number games

- electronic games
- record player
- records/cassettes/8-tracks
- musical instrument
- books
- hobby sets
- tickets to special event
- _____
- _____
- room furniture/accessories
- stereo/tape deck
- record/tape storage unit
- typewriter
- luggage
- journal
- manicure set
- hair blower/dryer
- grooming accessories
- hobby magazine/equipment/supplies

# ✓ Parents' Checklist for Child's Hospital Stay

- Help child know what to expect and be ready to answer his/her questions.

  ☐ Obtain specific information about illness or operation from pediatrician, surgeon, anesthesiologist:

      ___ approximate length of stay/recovery period
      ___ special tests/expected reactions
      ___ if surgery involved, type of anesthesia/how given/postoperative reactions
      ___ special diet considerations

  ☐ Find out procedures and routines from hospital admissions office and/or head pediatric nurse. Ask about:

      ___ preadmission tour/visit/written material on hospital life
      ___ rooming-in/stayover
      ___ parents' presence when anesthesia given/in recovery room
      ___ recovery room care
      ___ admissions day procedures
      ___ routine rests (blood/X rays)
      ___ visiting hours/rules
      ___ nursing shift hours or care by main nurse
      ___ wake-up/sleep/meal times
      ___ number of children in room
      ___ use of telephone/television
      ___ bringing security toys/pajamas
      ___ recreational facilities
      ___ school tutoring

  ☐ Get suggestions from your pediatrician on how and when to tell your child. Help allay fears:

      ___ answer questions truthfully and simply; be honest about pain involved
      ___ avoid promises you can't control
      ___ encourage child to talk about worst fears or act out with dolls, through drawings, or in a diary; be alert to child's misconceptions
      ___ explain that during operation s/he will not feel pain because s/he will be in a special sleep and will awaken in recovery room; you will be there or nearby

  ☐ Have child pack own suitcase if possible; have him/her choose homecoming outfit, take along family snapshots, toys, books, pajamas, toothbrush, school books, transistor radio.

☐ On arrival at hospital, explain unfamiliar sights:

    \_\_\_ IV stand
    \_\_\_ blood-pressure equipment
    \_\_\_ people hooked up to machines
    \_\_\_ wheeling stretchers
    \_\_\_ food tray trolleys
    \_\_\_ wheelchair
    \_\_\_ special beds
    \_\_\_ _____
    \_\_\_ _____

☐ When settling in child, explain the use of:

    \_\_\_ night light
    \_\_\_ nurse call button
    \_\_\_ control panel behind bed
    \_\_\_ automatic bed controls
    \_\_\_ bed pan/bathroom
    \_\_\_ eating/writing table
    \_\_\_ telephone
    \_\_\_ television

☐ Try to identify hospital personnel to child in terms of what they do:

    \_\_\_ pediatrician
    \_\_\_ anesthesiologist
    \_\_\_ floor nurses; head nurse
    \_\_\_ surgeon
    \_\_\_ intern(s)/resident(s)
    \_\_\_ lab technician(s)
    \_\_\_ dietician

### Things to Remember

- Arrange to be with child before and after operation and during new tests.

- Try to be there the same time every day . . . bring tape-recorded messages from siblings, friends . . . encourage other visitors such as relatives, teachers, baby-sitters.

- Let child know when you are going; never vanish without a good-bye . . . state firmly when you will return . . . leave something of yours or have favorite nurse there.

- Check medication and restrictions on eating so you can bring in acceptable treats.

- During recovery period, bring quiet easy games.

# ✓ Parents' Checklist for Baby-Sitter

- Have baby-sitter arrive to be with baby/child before s/he goes to sleep and before you leave.

- Let sitter know where you can be reached, when you expect to return.

- Discuss routine procedures:

  ☐ bedtime/naptime
  what hour . . . story . . . cuddle toy . . . stalling tricks . . . ventilation . . . covers . . . sleep position . . . how crib works.

  ☐ playtime
  acceptable games . . . TV limits . . . visiting with friends . . . clothing and rules for outdoor play.

  ☐ bathtime
  what hour . . . shampoo . . . special toys.

  ☐ feeding
  eating times . . . amounts . . . snacks/extra bottles . . . how to use equipment.

  ☐ occasional conditions
  thumbsucking . . . teething . . . baby/ child throws up . . . nightmares . . . child wakes up . . . tantrums . . . homework rules . . . visits by absent parent (divorced/separated spouse).

- Set ground rules for sitter:

  ☐ fees

  ☐ transportation arrangements

  ☐ kitchen privileges

  ☐ use of TV/stereo/telephone

  ☐ friends over to house

  ☐ smoking

  ☐ additional chores

- Provide household instructions:

  ☐ how you want telephone calls handled

  ☐ where emergency numbers are posted/extra cash kept

  ☐ what to do in case of accident/fire

  ☐ where to find kitchen/baby/household supplies

- Give sitter specific safety rules, especially for younger child:

  ☐ Do not leave youngsters alone in tub for any reason.

  ☐ Keep sharp objects, matches, medicines out of reach.

  ☐ Do not prop bottle up in crib; keep crib sides up.

  ☐ Keep cellar/garage door locked; remove toys from passageways.

  ☐ Hold child's hand at street crossings; keep in sight outdoors.

  ☐ Look in on sleeping baby often; make sure face is free of covers.

  ☐ Never open door for strangers or indicate over phone that parent is not at home.

  ☐ Note new skills of child (walking, stair climbing).

  ☐ Note any important medical handicaps or allergies.

147

# ✓ Checklist for Choosing a Camp

- Write or call for basic camp information:
  - ☐ location/distance from home
  - ☐ number of campers
  - ☐ accreditation
  - ☐ sessions (number of weeks)
  - ☐ costs
    - ____ per session/season
    - ____ special instruction/trips
    - ____ equipment/bedding rentals
    - ____ canteen money
    - ____ transportation/baggage shipping
    - ____ _____
  - ☐ makeup of camp
    - ____ age range
    - ____ all boys/all girls
    - ____ coed/brother-sister camps
    - ____ nonsectarian/religious
    - ____ private/sponsored
  - ☐ on-site recreation facilities
    - ____ swimming pool(s)/lake/boats
    - ____ stables
    - ____ playing fields/tennis courts
    - ____ archery/rifle ranges
    - ____ arts and crafts studio
    - ____ theater/stage
    - ____ indoor gym/social hall
    - ____ _____

- Consider child's major needs/wants in relation to camp goals, program and atmosphere:
  - ☐ Would child like to sample many different activities offered by a general camp? (The range of activities varies with individual camps.)
  - ☐ Would child like to concentrate on a special interest at a specialty camp? (Specialty camps offer intensive instruction in specific areas of interest.)
  - ☐ Does child need a camp that takes into account a special condition? (Some camps are geared to help with weight problems, physical handicaps, learning disabilities.)

- Interview camp director:
  - ☐ style of camp
    - ____ How structured is the program? Do children choose all/some/none of their activities?
    - ____ Are campers required to participate in specific activities?
    - ____ What is a typical daily schedule?
    - ____ How many children in a group activity?
    - ____ What are rainy day and evening activities?
    - ____ Is competition encouraged or played down?
    - ____ How does camp handle a homesick child?
    - ____ _____
  - ☐ sleeping/eating arrangements
    - ____ Do children sleep in bunks/tents?
    - ____ Number of campers and counselors in each bunk/tent?
    - ____ How many showers, toilets, sinks in bunk?
    - ____ What time is reveille, taps?
    - ____ What chores do campers perform?

___ Who does meal planning, preparation?

___ Is there provision for special dietary needs?

___ Are snack purchases monitored?

___ _____

☐ health/safety precautions

___ Is registered nurse on grounds? Who is in charge when s/he is off duty?

___ Is doctor on call? Where is hospital located?

___ Is parent told when child is admitted to infirmary?

___ Do waterfront counselors hold Red Cross or equivalent life-saving certificates?

___ What is the accident insurance coverage policy?

___ _____

☐ staff/camper background information

___ Is director the owner? Off-season occupation?

___ How long has camp been in existence? Under current owner?

___ Who is left in charge if director is away from camp?

___ How many counselors/campers return each year?

___ What is the counselor-camper ratio?

___ What is the age range of counselors?

___ What qualifications do general/specialty counselors have?

___ _____

☐ policies

___ How are telephone calls handled? Food packages from home?

___ Are children required to write home regularly?

___ What is visiting routine?

___ How do children get to and from camp?

___ What does camp do about smoking, drugs, drinking?

___ What about refunds?

___ _____

● Request names, telephone numbers of recent campers from your area. Talk to several and their parents.

☐ What features did you like best/least about camp?

☐ What are the counselors like?

☐ Do parents usually tip various counselors?

☐ How closely supervised are the campers?

☐ Is the camp schedule flexible?

☐ Is there a color war?

☐ How is the food? Second helpings allowed?

☐ Do a lot of kids get sick? Is infirmary well-run?

☐ How long have you been a camper there? Are you going back?

___ _____

___ _____

# ✓ Getting-Kids-Ready-for-Camp List

- Make doctor's appointment for checkup; see if booster shots are necessary.

- Fill out forms/sign and return to camp; note special instructions on medical form.

- Get camp rules on spending money, pets, "care packages," and telephone calls.

- Decide if you will deliver/pick up child or use camp transportation; notify camp.

- Have child try on clothes to see what fits; shop for needed items.

- Order name tapes; sew or press onto all clothing, bedding, linen and sleeping bag.

- Mark all belongings clearly: shoes, boots, rain gear, sports equipment, toilet articles, miscellaneous and optional items.

- Attach address tags to camp trunk and/or duffle bag; include name/ home address/phone number inside. (Spare set of trunk keys can be mailed to camp director.)

- Prepare bag lunch if needed for trip to camp; pack a travel bag with cards, book, pad, pencil.

- Reconfirm camp assembly point/time day before leaving.

- If child is going by public transportation, doublecheck that camp has arranged for his/her pickup at the other end. Give child a list with important telephone numbers and phone money in change.

- If you are driving child to camp, get exact directions, a road map, and arrive at suggested time.

## What to Bring (Suggested amounts will vary depending on camp/laundry.)

### Bedding and Linen
- ☐ twin-size sheets
- ☐ pillow cases
- ☐ pillow (if not supplied)
- ☐ heavy blankets
- ☐ light blankets
- ☐ bath towels
- ☐ washcloths
- ☐ laundry bag
- ☐ _____
- ☐ _____
- ☐ _____
- ☐ _____

### Clothing
- ☐ underwear
- ☐ T-shirts
- ☐ socks
- ☐ bathing suits
- ☐ shorts
- ☐ jeans
- ☐ belt(s)
- ☐ pajamas
- ☐ flannel pajamas
- ☐ sweaters
- ☐ heavy jacket
- ☐ sweatshirt
- ☐ flannel shirts
- ☐ terry robe
- ☐ dress outfit
- ☐ _____
- ☐ _____
- ☐ _____

- ☐ _____
- ☐ _____

### Rainwear
- ☐ raincoat/poncho
- ☐ rubber boots
- ☐ rain hat

### Footwear
- ☐ sneakers
- ☐ thongs
- ☐ walking/hiking shoes
- ☐ _____
- ☐ _____
- ☐ _____

### Toilet Articles
- ☐ toothbrush and container
- ☐ toothpaste
- ☐ comb and brush
- ☐ shampoo
- ☐ soap and soap dish
- ☐ plastic drinking cup
- ☐ facial tissues
- ☐ eyeglasses/prescription
- ☐ _____
- ☐ _____

### Miscellaneous
- ☐ flashlight/batteries
- ☐ sleeping bag
- ☐ ground cloth
- ☐ favorite soft toy
- ☐ stationery
- ☐ pens/pencils
- ☐ duplicate "What-to-Bring" list
- ☐ stamps

- ☐ insect repellent
- ☐ medication, labeled
- ☐ _____
- ☐ _____

### Optional
- ☐ nose/ear plugs
- ☐ swim cap
- ☐ Band-Aids
- ☐ sewing kit
- ☐ mess kit
- ☐ knapsack
- ☐ canteen
- ☐ _____
- ☐ _____
- ☐ _____
- ☐ baseball glove
- ☐ tennis racket/balls
- ☐ _____
- ☐ _____
- ☐ _____
- ☐ camera/film
- ☐ guitar
- ☐ _____
- ☐ books
- ☐ games/cards
- ☐ costume
- ☐ preaddressed/stamped envelopes
- ☐ _____
- ☐ _____
- ☐ _____
- ☐ _____

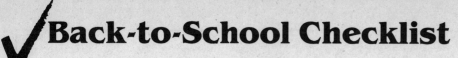

# Back-to-School Checklist

**Attend to Health/Personal Needs:**

☐ doctor's appointment

☐ update immunization records/fill out school medical forms

☐ dental checkup

☐ eye checkup

☐ fill eyeglass prescriptions

☐ get haircut

☐ fix up study area of room

☐ set ground rules for new school year

___ homework

___ TV

___ friends visiting

**Go Over Wardrobe:**

☐ see what has been outgrown

☐ mend/lengthen clothing

☐ make shopping list

___ outdoor wear

___ rain gear

___ classroom clothes/uniforms

___ dress clothes

___ underwear

___ shoes/socks

___ gym sneakers/shorts/leotards

___ _____

___ _____

___ _____

**Send in School Forms:**

☐ tuition payment/loan, if due

☐ medical forms

___ notification of special circumstances

☐ emergency telephone numbers

**Round Up School Supplies/Accessories:**

☐ notebooks/looseleaf/paper

☐ assignment pad

☐ pens/pencils/markers/crayons

☐ rulers/compass/erasers/sharpener

☐ textbook covers

☐ locker lock/key

☐ sports gear

☐ musical instrument

☐ lunchbox

☐ schoolbag/knapsack

☐ library card

☐ wallet/change purse

☐ extra house key

☐ watch

☐ books

☐ art supplies

**Arrange Schedule:**

☐ work out child-care hours

☐ arrange school transportation

___ train

___ bus

___ car pool

☐ enroll in after-school activities

___ music

___ dance

___ sports

___ _____

___ _____

☐ note special school events/holiday/ vacations on personal calendar

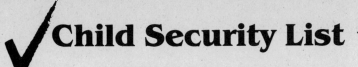 # Child Security List

**Going to and from School/Activities.**
**Advise Child:**

- Take the most traveled route and stick with it; avoid shortcuts through poorly lit areas, playing in deserted school yards, playgrounds, construction sites; stay away from bushes and doorways; walk purposefully, as if expected somewhere soon.

- Travel in groups; never go into public restroom, movie theater or amusement park alone.

- Avoid taking more money than is actually needed; do not flash new watch, pocket calculator, transistor radio, bus pass; keep pass in pocket until on bus.

- If followed, pretend to see a friend, wave and call out or change direction and run into a store or restaurant; scream to attract attention.

- Relinquish property if personal safety is threatened. Resist only if about to be hurt or kidnapped, then fight back in any way that gives a chance to break away and run for help. (If person is someone known, identify him/her to parents, teachers or police.)

- Notify parent or person in charge at home when going to be late or if plans are changed; give location and phone number, and if adult/parent will be present at party/sleepover.

- Never travel after dark without an adult or responsible teen.

**Dealing with Strangers.**
**Tell Child:**

- Do not stare at someone who behaves oddly; it may excite the person.

- Steer clear of talking to unknown adults.

- Never let a stranger touch your body; don't be frightened about reporting an adult who behaves oddly; try to remember details of the person's appearance.

- Check mirror before entering elevator to see if anyone is in corner; be wary of riding with a stranger; wait for next elevator.

- Never hitchhike or get into car with strangers; if someone tries to reach for you, run the opposite way from the direction of the moving car.

- Do not accept candy, presents or invitations from people you do not know; when trick-or-treating, do not enter homes or sample treats until they have been checked out at home.

- Don't open door when parents are not home; never reveal you are alone; keep door and windows locked; tell postman/delivery person to come back another time.

- Take telephone message without revealing parents' absence; say they cannot come to the phone right now but will call back soon if person leaves number. Don't tell your phone number or give any information over the phone.

### First Trip Alone

- Have child use means of transportation with an adult before going it alone (if possible). Be wary if child strongly objects to solo trip.

- Run through routine procedures (ticketing, boarding, meals, use of lavatory) as well as alternate procedures in case of delays or rerouting.

- Explain that if plane, train, bus is late arriving at destination, person meeting it will wait; provide additional contacts and telephone numbers for reassurance.

- Schedule travel during daylight; avoid weekend crowds.

- Tell child to sit near driver, conductor, flight attendant. Introduce child to this person if possible before you leave; make sure child knows how to make long-distance call, collect, and is carrying needed numbers and coins.

- Do not allow child to go unescorted at crowded urban bus/train terminals; arrange ahead for free services of Traveler's Aid Society worker who can meet child and stay with him/her while waiting for connecting transportation.

- Be available so that child can telephone you; check that s/he has reached destination.

# ✓ Checklist for a Teacher's Conference

- Look over schoolwork your child has brought home. Note:

  ☐ changes in marks

  ☐ changes in skills

  ☐ teacher's comments

  ☐ what is being tested

  ☐ _____

- Talk to child about school. Ask about:

  ☐ scholastic activities that are learning experiences

  ☐ subjects likes most/why

  ☐ subjects likes least/why

  ☐ subjects finds hardest/why

  ☐ homework, completed and handed in

  ☐ getting along with teacher(s)

  ☐ getting along with classmates

  ☐ _____

- Ask Teacher:*

  ☐ Is child working above/below/on grade level? (Look at child's class work.)

*As suggested by the National Committee for Citizens in Education

☐ What are child's strengths/weaknesses/special talents?

☐ Is homework in and completed on time?

☐ Does child show initiative and ask questions when in doubt?

☐ How does child get along with classmates/teacher(s)?

☐ How does child score on standardized tests?

☐ What do the results mean?

☐ Is remedial work advised? Should parent work with child? In what ways?

☐ How much time is child expected to spend on homework each night?

☐ Has child's grasp of work grown/stayed the same/declined?

☐ Does child need any special guidance? Visits with school counselor? Do study habits need improving?

☐ Does s/he recommend fewer outside activities?

☐ Has s/he noticed any changes that might indicate a health-related problem?

☐ Is any special program or placement suggested for next year?

## Outcome of Conference

- Sum up goals both parent and teacher are working toward.

- Discuss ways you can work with child without exerting undue pressure.

- If you haven't understood something, ask teacher to explain or give you examples of what s/he suggests.

- If you wish to review your child's school records, say so. (You may be required to make a separate appointment and/or submit a written statement explaining items to which you object.)

- Involve child in setting up goals and plans for improving work/attitude.

- Set date for follow-up parent-teacher conference; allow time to implement suggestions made.

# ✔ Checklist for Choosing a College

- Why do you want to go to college?

- What type of environment would be most beneficial?

☐ Figure out the aspects of college that are most important to you:

___ intellectual atmosphere
___ active extracurricular program
___ independent study and research
___ strong academic reputation
___ technical training
___ vocational experience
___ placement in graduate schools
___ chance to interact with faculty
___ variety of social activities
___ homogeneous/diverse groups
___ politically active student body
___ size of college population
___ traditional/innovative study program
___ strong reputation for specific field of study

___ _____

☐ Get basic information from catalogs, high school guidance office, admissions office:

___ location
   ☐ distance from home

   ☐ urban/suburban/rural campus

   ☐ nearness to cultural or other facilities

   ☐ _____

___ type of school
   ☐ denominational/nonsectarian

   ☐ state supported/private

   ☐ liberal arts/professional

   ☐ _____

___ student population
   ☐ size

   ☐ makeup (geographic, ethnic, racial, religious, economic)

   ☐ male/female ratio

   ☐ number of undergraduates/graduates living on/off campus

   ☐ percentage of commuter students

   ☐ _____

___ academic qualifications
   ☐ accreditation

   ☐ range of freshman SAT scores

   ☐ number of Merit scholars who have attended

   ☐ selectivity of admissions board

   ☐ percentage of students entering graduate schools

   ☐ ratio of faculty to students

   ☐ faculty member degrees, publications

   ☐ _____

___ library facilities
   ☐ ratio of books to students

   ☐ location of library(s) on campus

   ☐ hours open

   ☐ research/specialty libraries/periodicals/microfilm/data processing

   ☐ access to stacks/study carrels

   ☐ _____

___ special undergraduate programs
   ☐ cross-registration in neighboring colleges

   ☐ percentage of required/elective courses for degree

☐ work-study program

☐ study abroad

☐ three-year degree

☐ interdepartmental majors

☐ career credits

☐ _____

___ costs

☐ tuition

☐ room and board

☐ books/lab fees

☐ travel expenses

☐ personal living expenses (laundry, recreation)

☐ financial aid available

☐ _____

___ housing facilities

☐ on-campus housing guaranteed for four years

☐ co-ed dorms/male-female only dorms

☐ married students dorm

☐ off-campus housing (provided by college, by student, transportation)

☐ fraternity/sorority housing

☐ _____

___ medical facilities

☐ student infirmary

☐ counseling services

☐ insurance coverage

☐ nearest hospital/dental facility

☐ nurse/doctor on campus

☐ _____

___ religious facilities

☐ town churches/synagogues

☐ campus religious clubs

☐ nonsectarian facility on campus

☐ _____

___ extracurricular facilities

☐ intra/extra-mural sports

☐ student newspaper/magazine/radio/TV station

☐ social activity centers (student union, fraternity/sorority houses)

☐ campus theater/movie houses

☐ music/dance groups

☐ _____

☐ _____

☐ _____

☐ _____

___ campus policies and regulations

☐ dorms (curfews, co-ed visiting, roommate requests)

☐ classes/grades (change of major or school, attendance, pass/fail option)

☐ cars (campus registration, university parking permit)

☐ drinking/smoking/drugs

☐ tuition payment extension/refunds

☐ _____

☐ _____

☐ _____

☐ Meet with representatives of various colleges, students attending, alumni; ask about aspects of college important to you.

☐ Plan to visit several colleges before accepting any; try to see school when it is in session. When visiting:

___ look at dorms closely—rooms, bathrooms, dining rooms

___ sit in on classes

___ talk to faculty member in your potential field

___ walk around campus

☐ Speak to students informally. Ask their opinions about:

___ special requirements for freshmen

___ academics

___ faculty

___ social activities

___ campus politics

___ expenses

___ student attitudes

☐ Compare all information about colleges in terms of your priorities. Keep in mind that your favorite colleges may not accept you; all your college choices need to be weighed carefully.

# ✓Off-to-College List

☐ **For Room**

___ curtains

___ bedspread/comforter/blankets

___ pillow/linens

___ throw pillows

___ desk/chair

___ reading chair

___ bookshelves

___ storage drawers/hangers

___ rug

___ lamps/extension cords

___ posters/pictures

___ telephone

___ portable refrigerator

___ TV/stereo/tape recorder

___ clock/radio/alarm

___ hotpot/immersion cord

___ _____ ___ _____

___ _____ ___ _____

☐ **Important Papers**

___ medical forms/shot records

___ prescriptions

___ birth certificate

___ school I.D.

___ car registration

___ driver's license

___ college parking permit

___ working papers

___ checkbook/savings passbook

___ credit/charge cards

___ campus bookstore charge

___ cash

___ telephone/address book

___ photos

___ _____ ___ _____

___ _____

☐ **For School**

___ typewriter/paper/carbons

___ notebooks/pads/pens

___ stapler/scissors/tape

___ dictionary/thesaurus

___ textbooks

___ _____ ___ _____

___ _____ ___ _____

☐ **For Wardrobe**

___ garment bags

___ school clothes

___ sport clothes/gear

___ knockaround clothes

___ weather gear (cold/warm)

___ going-out clothes

___ travel iron

___ _____ ___ _____

___ _____ ___ _____

☐ **Personal Items**

___ grooming supplies

___ sewing kit

___ first-aid kit

___ musical instrument

___ camera/film

___ stationery/stamps

___ board games

___ sports equipment

# Your Health

☐ **Health Insurance Checklist**

☐ **Things to Do Before Going into the Hospital**

☐ **Medical Records List**

☐ **Early Warning Signals Checklist**

☐ **Checklist for Choosing a Doctor**

☐ **Checklist for Reducing Stress**

☐ **The Ultimate Drug-Store List**

☐ **Checklist for Choosing a Nursing Home**

☐ **Dieter's Checklist**

# ✓Health Insurance Checklist

☐ Check the benefits under your policies to see if they are reasonable in relation to current hospital and doctor costs in your community.

☐ See who is covered by the policy and for how long:

___ children over 18

___ maternity benefits

___ over 65

☐ Find out under what conditions your policy may be cancelled and/or renewed (for you and for the insurance company). Note:

___ grace period for late payments of premiums

___ physical examination requirements, if any; under what circumstances

☐ Know what services/conditions are excluded in the policy:

___ dental work

___ optical expenses

___ maternity/abortion expenses

___ private nursing

___ convalescent stays in nursing home

___ chronic alcoholism

___ drug addiction

___ any preexisting conditions

☐ Check the insurance company's policy on refusing benefits for preexisting conditions.

## Types of Coverage

☐ Hospital Expense Insurance

___ Does it pay a set amount per day toward room and board? Or a percentage of the hospital stay?

___ What is the maximum number of days allowed?

___ When does payment take place?

___ What is included in the basic charges for hospital services (besides room and board)?

- lab tests

- X rays

- drugs/medication

- use of operating room

- anesthesia and administration

- local ambulance service

- minor medical supplies

- general nursing care

☐ Surgical Expense Insurance

___ How much is allotted for each surgical procedure?

___ Is there coverage for surgery not performed in a hospital?

___ Are outpatient recovery charges included?

___ Is anesthesia covered?

___ Is there a maximum dollar amount specified in the policy or does it pay a percentage of surgeon's fee?

☐ Medical Expense Insurance

___ What is the payment coverage for non-surgical doctor bills?

- regular visits to doctor's office

- visits to specialists

- house calls

- hospital visits

☐ Major Medical Insurance

___ How well does it cover prolonged illness costs? Does it pick up where your basic coverage stops?

_____ What is the deductible? Is there a new deductible for each new illness?

_____ What percentage of your bills does policy pay? Or is there a maximum dollar amount stated after which you will not be responsible? After recovery, will the maximum amount again be available?

_____ When does coverage start?

_____ Does coverage stop after a certain time period in hospital? Or will payment stop after the dollar amount of policy has been reached?

_____ What services are included?

- out-of-hospital expenses/treatments
- private nursing care
- surgical appliances
- surgery
- radiation therapy
- obstetric services
- psychiatric treatment
- drugs
- X rays
- specified ambulance services
- home health care/nursing home care

☐ Disability Insurance

_____ How does your policy define "disability" and the extent of your incapacity to work?

_____ What proportion of your regular earning is paid?

_____ How much time elapses before insurance takes effect? Is it retroactive?

_____ What is the duration of the benefits?

## Before You Buy

- Evaluate the health services that are available to you and your family and the health history of your family.

- Look into group policies open to you; supplement with individual policies if necessary.

- Check that policies don't overlap; spouse's office coverage may include workmen's compensation, disability provisions.

- Consider buying a policy that pays a percentage of fees rather than one that pays fixed amounts.

- Note that you can reduce your premiums with a higher deductible and longer time-deferred payment.

- Find out the waiting period before a policy becomes effective and benefits begin.

- Look into new types of coverage for special family needs: prepaid group health plans, dental expense insurance, school insurance for children, travel accident, special hazards.

- Compare rates and payment records of companies in your area; check state insurance departments for record to find out if company is licensed to do business in your state.

# ✓ Things to Do Before Going into the Hospital

### Talk to Your Doctor

☐ Ask your doctor to outline the tests s/he has ordered for you, what they entail and the reasons for them.

☐ Find out if any tests can be done before you are admitted to the hospital. Take the results of such tests with you, if possible, or have your doctor notify the hospital that you have already taken them.

☐ Check out anesthetic and nursing practices if going in for surgery; ask if postoperative private-duty nurse is recommended; follow procedures for getting one if needed.

☐ Note any diet restrictions or special medications the doctor has ordered.

### Speak with Hospital Personnel

☐ Examine your insurance to see what type of room is covered and for how long; decide if you want to reserve a private/semi-private or room with more people in it.

☐ Call the admitting office to place your request and ask about:

____ insurance documentation required
____ admitting time and procedures (Can you telephone in information to facilitate the check-in process?)
____ visiting hours/having own telephone/TV/paper delivered

☐ Discuss the type of insurance you have and what fees/services/medications it will/will not cover; clarify what charges must be paid before you can be released from the hospital.

☐ Assemble insurance/medical data you need to bring:

____ health insurance card
____ medicare/medicaid I.D.
____ social security number
____ a list of all medications you take regularly (and those you have taken within the last two weeks, including diuretic/aspirin)
____ medical history of you/your family
____ names/addresses/telephone numbers of persons to notify in case of emergency

## Make Personal Arrangements

☐ Decide how available you want to be while in the hospital; notify only those people you wish to see or speak to about your upcoming stay; leave instructions on how to handle others.

☐ Provide trusted friend or relative with signed checks for private nursing care/rent/other bill payments.

☐ Arrange to have your telephone messages and mail delivered in person or kept in a safe place until you return.

☐ Notify your employer of hospitalization/recuperation time; arrange essential coverage of your work; tie up loose ends if time permits.

☐ Update your will and letter of instruction if necessary.

☐ Check your calendar in the office and at home to see if any appointments need to be rescheduled or tickets disposed of or exchanged.

☐ Cancel newspaper delivery; arrange pet and plant care if no one else will be home.

☐ Arrange housekeeping/baby-sitting help, if needed; post daily routine with clear instructions. (You may want to cook/freeze ahead.)

☐ Post important telephone numbers; make sure each family member and housekeeper know where they are. Call from hospital and leave your phone number as soon as you know it.

## Packing Up

___ hairbrush/comb

___ toothbrush/paste

___ deodorant

___ shaving supplies

___ cologne

___ hand or body lotion/makeup

___ shower cap

___ pajamas or nightgowns

___ personal pillow/case

___ bathrobe/slippers

___ glasses/contacts and cleaning case

___ minimal cash ($10 or less/ leave valuables in safe-deposit box)

___ stationery/stamps

___ telephone/address book

___ books/TV guide

___ transistor radio

___ paperwork

# Medical Records List

- Keep this list up-to-date and in your household records file along with all health insurance data.

- List doctors and medical facilities you use regularly; note names/addresses/telephone numbers and specialties.

  - health-care center
  - hospital
  - family doctor

  - surgeon
  - pediatrician
  - eye doctor

  - dentist
  - _____
  - _____

**Personal Records**

Your birth date:

Your blood type:

Your allergies/sensitivities: (onset date/special conditions, medications/emergency procedures)

Childhood diseases: (names/age at which you had them)

Other dated records:

___ major illnesses (treatment/doctor/hospital)

___ surgical operations/pregnancies
     (doctor/hospital)

___ major injuries

___ adult immunizations (for travel, etc.)

___ medications/drugs (taken within last year)

___ results of health checkups

  - weight/height
  - blood pressure
  - blood test results
  - _____
  - _____
  - _____

___ eye checkups
  - glaucoma test results
  - copy of prescription glasses
  - vision with/without glasses
  - _____

___ dental checkups
  - conditions (cavity-prone/gums/braces)
  - mouth surgery (type/doctor)
  - _____

## For Children

Birth date:

Blood type:

Allergies/sensitivities: (onset date/special conditions, medications/emergency procedures)

Dated records:

____ height/weight

____ medications/drugs (taken within last year)

____ immunizations (include boosters)
- DT or DPT
- tetanus booster
- rubella
- measles
- mumps
- polio
- TB test

____ childhood diseases (special aftereffects, if any)

- chicken pox
- _____
- _____

____ major illnesses/infections (special after effects, if any)
- tonsilitis
- whooping cough
- influenza
- pneumonia
- hepatitis
- rheumatic fever
- _____
- _____

____ fractures/major injuries (where on body)

____ surgical operations (type/doctor/hospital)

____ eye checkups
- vision (with/without glasses)
- copy of prescription
- _____

____ dental checkups
- conditions (prone to cavities/braces)
- mouth surgery (type/doctor)
- _____

## Family Medical History

List blood relatives (starting with grandparents) and note:

____ health habits (smoking/drinking, etc.)

____ major disorders/illnesses/age at onset
- diabetes
- heart disease
- cancer (type)
- hypertension
- kidney disease
- arthritis (type)
- respiratory/emphysema
- tuberculosis
- anemia
- nervous system disorders
- epilepsy/seizures
- stomach disorders
- cataracts/glaucoma
- psychiatric problems
- _____

____ birth defects

____ age at death

____ cause of death

# Early Warning Signals Checklist

Three of the most common killers in this country are heart disease, cancer and stroke. Do you know the early warning signs that should act as an alert for prompt medical diagnosis?

## Cancer

- unusual bleeding or discharge

- sore that does not heal within two weeks

- change in bowel or bladder habits, persistent cramps

- thickening or lump in breast or elsewhere in body

- noticeable change in size or color of wart or mole

- hoarseness or nagging cough that lasts beyond two weeks

- problem with swallowing or indigestion that persists

## Stroke

- sudden, temporary weakness or numbness of face, arm or leg

- paralysis of face, arm or leg, especially localized on one side

- temporary difficulty with speech

- intense headache

- brief dimness or loss of vision in one or both eyes

- double vision

- temporary dizziness or unsteadiness

- loss of memory

- change in personality or mental ability

- loss of consciousness

- signs may last from fifteen minutes to several hours

## Heart Attack

- intense pressure, piercing pain, tightness, burning or squeezing inward feeling in middle chest

- chest pains may last minutes, hours or be intermittent

- chest pains may travel to one or both arms, to

the shoulders, neck or jaws, and may or may not be accompanied by:

\_\_\_ shortness of breath

\_\_\_ weakness, tiredness, faintness, paleness

\_\_\_ nausea, vomiting

\_\_\_ heavy, cold sweating

# ✓ Checklist for Choosing a Doctor

- Get recommendations from hospitals and other doctors; check out credentials in state medical directory (available in libraries):

    ☐ What specialty board certification does s/he have?

    ☐ How long has doctor been in practice? What medical school attended/internships/residencies?

    ☐ What hospital(s) is s/he affiliated with?

    ☐ Is s/he on the teaching or research staff?

    ☐ What do other doctors think of him/her? Does s/he keep up with latest available medical information?

- Ask people who are patients of the doctor:

    ☐ Is s/he a good diagnostician? Thorough?

    ☐ How does s/he handle an emergency/hospitalized patients?

    ☐ Is the office well-equipped? Are good records kept?

    ☐ Does doctor give patient information such as results of tests/lab reports/medication side effects?

    ☐ Does doctor have a reputation for being an "alarmist"/overprescribing medication/speaking in medical jargon/not returning calls?

    ☐ Is it easy to get appointments? How long are office waits?

    ☐ Does the doctor treat men and women the same? Is s/he sympathetic and easy to talk to?

    ☐ Does s/he answer questions/go beyond the immediate problem to look at the whole?

    ☐ When s/he is not available, who is the covering doctor?

    ☐ How does fee schedule compare with other doctors in area?

    ☐ What do you like most/least about this doctor? How long have you used him/her?

- Check out doctor's policy on:

    ☐ making house calls

    ☐ prescribing over the telephone

    ☐ second opinions

    ☐ controversial treatments

    ☐ coverage during days off/vacation

    ☐ filling out insurance forms

- Note convenience factors:

    ☐ distance of office from your home/means of getting there

    ☐ location of affiliated hospital

    ☐ office hours

**Choosing a Pediatrician**

- Get recommendations from your obstetrician, children's hospital, parents. (Location of doctor's office and affiliated hospital may be a greater consideration.)

- Check out doctor's credentials, policies and reputation among parents. In addition to the aforementioned questions, ask:

  - ☐ Is s/he sympathetic to first-time parents?
  - ☐ Does the doctor have a good rapport with children? Is not condescending? Takes time to answer their questions?
  - ☐ How is s/he in an emergency? How is doctor who covers for him/her?
  - ☐ Does s/he have specific telephone hours during day to discuss problems?

- Find out view on subjects about which parents and/or pediatricians may disagree:

  - ☐ breast/bottle feeding/eating routines/vitamins
  - ☐ toilet training/bedwetting
  - ☐ pacifiers/thumbsucking
  - ☐ rooming-in with hospitalized child
  - ☐ full-time working mothers
  - ☐ sex roles
  - ☐ _____
  - ☐ _____

- Afterward, ask yourself:

  - ☐ Did you feel rushed?
  - ☐ Were you encouraged to give your point of view? Free to disagree?
  - ☐ How were incoming calls handled while you were in the office?
  - ☐ Do his/her childrearing ideas seem similar to yours? If not, would you still feel comfortable using him/her?

# ✓ Checklist for Reducing Stress

☐ Get up twenty minutes earlier in the morning for a hassle-free start on the day.

☐ Set realistic daily goals; assume some tasks will not be completed; take breaks from work no matter how busy you are.

☐ Include a physical fitness routine in your daily and weekly schedule.

☐ Trust your instincts more often; make sure your values, not someone else's, determine your living standard.

☐ Take it one step at a time when you feel pressured to get things done; focus on what you are doing rather than how you are doing it.

☐ Recognize that changes, happy or sorrowful, often trigger anxiety; practice relaxing when you feel tense wherever you are—stretch, breathe deeply, reflect quietly.

☐ Diffuse anger by working it off in a physical activity.

☐ Shorten fretful waiting times by bringing along something you enjoy: a good book, newspaper, needlepoint.

☐ Cultivate a hobby you can grow with and keep developing.

☐ Try to understand the other person's point of view before rejecting it; give others a chance to have the last word.

☐ Accept that mistakes happen and that you are never going to be perfect; learn to laugh at your shortcomings; rely on a sense of humor to deal with what you cannot control or change.

# ✓ The Ultimate Drug-Store List

## Health and Drug Items

___ thermometer

___ Vaseline

___ antiseptic ointments

___ peroxide

___ Band-Aids

___ burn ointments

___ gauze pads/adhesive tape

___ zinc oxide ointment

___ boric acid

___ _____

___ _____

___ antihistamines

___ cough syrup/lozenges

___ sore-throat medication

___ cold tablets/liquids

___ nasal spray/drops

___ aspirin/aspirin substitutes

___ allergy medications

___ _____

___ _____

___ _____

___ alcohol

___ Epsom salts

___ distilled water

___ sterile cotton

___ salt tablets

___ vitamin/mineral tablets

___ athletic bandages

___ heating pad (wet/dry)

___ ice pack

___ _____

___ _____

___ lip balm ointment

___ sun block/screen

___ calamine lotion

___ acne medication

___ astringent

___ dandruff/shampoo medication

___ _____

___ _____

___ laxatives/ suppositories

___ mineral oil

___ Kaopectate

___ prepacked enema bottles

___ hemorrhoid medication

___ diuretics

___ _____

___ muscle-pain ointment

___ corn plasters/removers

___ _____

___ _____

___ toothache/mouth medication

___ eye drops

___ medicated powders (foot)

___ _____

___ sanitary supplies

___ contraceptive devices

___ pregnancy test kits

___ _____

___ _____

___ surgical supplies

___ _____

___ prescription medications

___ _____

___ _____

___ _____

___ _____

___ _____

___ _____

## Grooming and Beauty Items

___ toothbrush

___ toothpaste/powder

___ dental floss/pick

___ gum stimulators

___ denture gripper/cleanser

___ mouthwash

___ _____

___ _____

___ shampoo

___ comb/brush/pick

___ hair blower

___ hair sprays

___ hair coloring

___ permanent kits

___ hair conditioners

___ bobby pins/hair pins

___ hair rollers

___ barettes/combs

___ _____

___ _____

___ _____

___ tissues/cotton swabs

___ bath soap

___ scrub brush

___ shower cap

___ body lotion/cream

___ bath powder

___ bubble bath

___ _____

___ _____

___ pumice stone

___ nail clippers/scissors

___ cuticle nippers/manicure
    kit

___ nail file/emery boards

___ polish remover

___ hand cream

___ _____

___ _____

___ shaving cream

___ razor/blades

___ after-shave lotion/cream

___ styptic pencil

___ depilatory cream/wax

___ facial hair bleach

___ _____

___ _____

___ cosmetics

  • eye shadow
  • lipstick
  • powder
  • base makeup
  • mascara
  • eyeliner
  • face creams/oils
  • _____
  • _____
  • _____

___ antiperspirant/deodorant

___ suntan lotion/cream/oil

___ _____

___ _____

___ cold cream

___ perfume/toilet water

___ cosmetic bags

___ shaving kits

___ _____

___ _____

___ _____

___ _____

___ _____

___ _____

___ _____

___ _____

___ _____

___ _____

# ✔ Checklist for Choosing a Nursing Home

Evaluate the needs of the individual to determine the appropriate type of facility* as directed by your doctor. Would the individual need:

- ☐ skilled nursing facility for patients (SNF)
  - ___ around-the-clock nursing care
  - ___ special diets
  - ___ medical exam within 48 hours after admittance
  - ___ medical services (lab tests, X rays)
  - ___ rehabilitative therapies
  - ___ regular recreation program
- ☐ intermediate-care facility for those with chronic conditions (ICF)
  - ___ continuous personal care
  - ___ medical supervision
  - ___ assistance with routine daily needs
  - ___ social facilities
  - ___ activity programs
- ☐ residential (domiciliary)-care facility for group living in a sheltered environment
  - ___ continuing care basis
  - ___ medical monitoring
  - ___ recreational opportunities/programs
  - ___ housekeeping services

Find out about appropriate homes available to the individual. Have you looked into:

- ☐ recommendations
  - ___ individual's doctor
  - ___ social services department of hospital
  - ___ community service directory (local library)
  - ___ religious organizations
  - ___ state health care associations
  - ___ senior citizen center/agency on aging
- ☐ location convenience
  - ___ to hospital/other medical facilities
  - to your home/office/other family members

*Regulatory laws, certification, service requirements, and eligibility for certain programs vary from one type of facility to another as well as from state to state.

- ___ to public transportation
- ___ to shopping
- ☐ accreditation
  - ___ current state license or certification
  - ___ administrator's license or certification/qualifications
  - ___ staff qualifications
- ☐ costs
  - ___ basic daily/monthly charges/extras
  - ___ Medicare/Medicaid coverage

Visit several nursing homes of your choice. Did you look closely at:

- ☐ physical facilities
  - ___ buildings well-maintained/clean
  - ___ layout planned for the elderly/infirm
    - • grab bars
    - • wide doorways
    - • ample elevators
    - • nonskid floors/ramps
    - • tables accommodating wheelchairs
  - ___ outdoor area
  - ___ separate rooms for contagious patients/medical exams/therapy/social activities
  - ___ fire safety exits/emergency evacuation
- ☐ rooms
  - ___ cheerful/adequate space (maximum four to a room)
  - ___ single rooms available
  - ___ locked closet or dresser/adequate space
  - ___ easy access to beds (not cots)
  - ___ provision for privacy (visits/phone calls)
  - ___ residents bring some of their own furniture/possessions
  - ___ emergency buzzers within reach of each resident
- ☐ food and diet
  - ___ registered dietician on staff
  - ___ clean/well-run kitchen
  - ___ food attractive/nutritious; prepared/served well

____ snacks available

____ residents keep own food in storage/re-frigerated area

____ cheerful/well-run dining room

Speak to administrator about operational services and policies. Have you discussed thoroughly:

☐ administration and staff

____ who owns home (note any conflict of in-terests)

____ owner-operated home

____ staff belongs to union

____ language barrier between staff and res-idents

____ adequate/qualified staff to care for res-idents

____ community volunteers performing regu-lar services

☐ medical and nursing services

____ full/part-time staff physician

____ regular medical checkups/how often

____ medical director on staff/qualified in ge-riatric medicine

____ complete/accurate records kept/can be reviewed by family

____ trained/adequate nursing staff

____ who administers drugs/injections

____ emergency admission arrangements at nearby hospital

____ physical therapy and/or other rehabili-tation available

____ dental/pharmacy/podiatry/optometrist services available

☐ activities

____ varied activities daily (group or individ-ual)

____ outside trips

____ residents participate in planning

____ religious programs (note emphasis)

____ free to visit relatives/friends/go shop-ping

☐ individual residency policies

____ handle own money/mail/phone

____ married couples permitted to room to-gether

____ choose own doctor(s)

____ visiting hours/special rules/young chil-dren permitted

____ roommate selection

____ informing resident/family members of health condition

☐ costs and expenses

____ Medicare/Medicaid/old-age assistance financing available (home helps apply for these benefits)

____ initial entry fee

____ regular financial accounting (monthly statement)

____ refund of advances if patient leaves/dies

____ extra charges

● medications

● special diet

● incontinence

● dental/eye/foot care

● physical therapy

● bedridden services/private nurses

● special medical equipment/supplies

● personal grooming (haircut/shave)

● _____

Observe residents and staff attitudes closely; speak to residents and their families. Note:

____ doors to rooms always kept open (easy on nurses)

____ uneaten food on many plates in dining room (patients need more help/food not tasty)

____ staff clustered in small groups

____ number of patients restrained/sedated

____ how residents are groomed

____ how quickly staff responds to resident calls

____ interest/time given to residents by staff

____ ethnic/religious makeup of home

____ state of health of residents

____ compatibility of residents

____ busy/satisfied/well-cared-for residents

When you decide upon a nursing home, don't sign any entrance contract or other document be-fore checking it out with your lawyer.

# ✔ Dieter's Checklist

Check whatever diet plan you follow with your family doctor and remind yourself daily: you are the only person who can control what you eat. Note the following strategies:

- Set a return-visit date the same time you set weight-loss goals with your doctor; give away clothes as they get big on you; assume they will never fit you again.

- Post a copy of your diet on the refrigerator door; slip another in your wallet/purse; tack a favorite picture of yourself when slimmer to your mirror next to a current snapshot.

- Keep a calorie counter within easy reach; list calories of foods most tempting to you and try to keep them out of the house. (An empty cookie jar offers no temptation.)

- Record everything you eat in a special notebook; use a pocket calculator to tally a day's calories; note under what circumstances you crave certain foods or start to overeat.

- Weigh yourself on a reliable scale not more often than once a week; do it before you get dressed in the morning; expect to drop pounds gradually; keep track of lost inches by using a tape measure.

- Work some kind of physical exercise into your daily routine; try to walk more, climb stairs; develop a new interest that is very satisfying.

- Use low-calorie substitutes whenever possible; measure amounts with a food scale, pour drinks with a shot glass; trim extra fat from meat before you cook; use a nonstick spray coat to cut down on cooking oil.

- Eat more often but less of everything; cut food into small portions; enjoy little bits of goodies so you don't feel totally deprived.

- Figure out a day's menu that enables the whole family to enjoy shared meals; encourage children to clear their plates away so leftovers are thrown out before you can get at them.

- Stock refrigerator with prepared-ahead diet nibbles (protein snacks, crisp raw vegetables); plan what you will eat before you go into a restaurant.

- Drink water between and before meals; eat only when sitting at the table (even when snacking); eat salad first when you are hungriest; eat chicken without the skin on it.

- Take time to taste what you put into your mouth; chew slowly; pause between mouthfuls; put fork down after each bite; try to leave something on your plate.

- Concentrate on sticking to your diet one day at a time; make up for a lapse by eating less next time rather than giving up.

# Personal Matters

☐ **Wedding Plan List**

☐ **Gift Idea List**

☐ **Gift Giver's Holiday Checklist**

☐ **The Ultimate Hobby List**

☐ **Things to Do When Wallet/Purse Is Lost**

☐ **Things to Consider Before Remarrying**

☐ **Personal Safety Checklist**

☐ **Your Official Numbers List**

☐ **List of Important Dates for Your Calendar**

☐ **Your Personal Checklist**

# ✔ Wedding Plan List

Have you made a list of anticipated expenses?

---- officiating fee

---- space rentals

---- bridal party gifts

---- flowers/bouquets

---- invitations/announcements

---- stationery/postage

---- gown/accessories

---- trousseau

---- going-away outfit

---- barber/hairdresser

---- ring(s)

---- food/drink

---- rentals

---- wedding cake

---- catering services

---- photographer

---- album/copies

---- music

---- transportation

---- lodging for out-of-town wedding party

---- medical tests

---- marriage license

---- prewedding parties

## Six to Eight Months Before the Wedding

☐ Decide type and size of wedding you want; figure the more formal, the more time and money you will need.

☐ Set date and time; check that clergy person/judge will be available; find out regulations that may apply.

☐ Decide where you want to hold the wedding/reception:

---- church/synagogue
---- hotel/club
---- catering hall
---- private home/garden
---- nontraditional setting

☐ For church/synagogue wedding, look into arrangements for:

---- floral decorations
---- music/choir/soloist
---- seating gueats
---- transportation to and from for members of wedding party, photographer

☐ For wedding and/or reception held at club/hotel/catering hall, be prepared to reserve space six months in advance. Insist on prices in writing with itemized services; find out what happens if you have to cancel before you sign any contracts.

☐ Compare several locations, transportation, menu costs, what is included in the wedding package. Find out arrangements for:

---- dressing room
---- coat check
---- parking facilities
---- bar service
---- hors d'oeuvres
---- wedding cake
---- floral decorations
---- table seating/settings
---- printed matches/menus

☐ For a wedding and/or reception held in a home or garden, look into services you will need, items to purchase separately (such as wines/liquor/ice cubes) and exactly what each service provides; what the extras are:

\_\_\_\_ caterer (menu plans/cake)

\_\_\_\_ bartender/serving help (number/what jobs performed)

\_\_\_\_ florist (extent of floral arrangements/who sets up)

\_\_\_\_ rental services

- dishes
- flatware
- glasses
- linens
- tables
- tents
- canopy
- coat racks
- setting up

☐ Choose attendants; purchase/wrap gifts to give bridesmaids, maid/matron of honor, best man, ushers, flower girl/boy

☐ Make out guest list; obtain one from bridegroom's family. Note who is to be invited to wedding, reception, or both, and who is to receive announcements only.

☐ Order invitations, announcements, and thank-you notes from recommended stationer; get delivery dates.

☐ Shop for wedding dress, bridal veil and other accessories; arrange for fittings.

☐ Coordinate bridal party clothes; dye items that need to be the same color (shoes/head-pieces) at the same time.

☐ Help mother of the bride select her dress and inform bridegroom's mother of style, color, length.

☐ Engage photographer; look at portfolio and select type of photographs and style of al-

bums; discuss arrangements for taking: bridal and family portraits, prewedding photos, ceremony, receiving line and reception photos.

☐ See florist about all floral decorations in home, synagogue/church, and at club or hotel; note flowers to be worn or carried at wedding.

☐ Decide on musicians/music for ceremony/reception; discuss fees and playing times.

☐ Plan wardrobe for wedding trip; shop for trousseau.

**A Month Before the Wedding**

☐ Address envelopes.

☐ Mail invitations.

☐ Notify newspapers of engagement.

☐ Get wedding form from newspaper.

☐ Select wedding ring(s).

☐ Arrange lodging, meals, transportation for out-of-town members of the wedding party.

☐ Get medical tests.

☐ Obtain marriage license. Bring necessary documents.

☐ Order wedding cake.

**The Last Week**

☐ Set up rehearsal times and inform wedding party.

☐ Notify caterer/hotel of number attending.

☐ Doublecheck details, delivery places and dates.

☐ Pack for wedding trip.

☐ Inform attendants of dressing arrangements.

☐ Leave extra time to dress and have pictures taken before leaving for ceremony.

# ✓ Gift Idea List

## For the Home: Indoor

---- lucky horseshoe

---- doormat

---- coat tree

---- umbrella stand

---- luggage rack

---- magazine rack

---- bookends

---- reference books

---- antique whatnots

---- decorative boxes

---- ash trays

---- incense/holder

---- lamp

---- decorative extension cords

---- planters

---- plants/flowers

---- vase

---- throw pillows

---- afghan

---- poster

---- etchings

---- picture frame

---- sculpture

---- fireplace accessories
- bellows
- long matches
- 

---- cord of wood

---- log tote/roller

---- corn popper

---- bar accessories*

---- stereo/headphones

---- portable television

---- tape recorder/tapes

---- rolling file

---- telephone-answering machine

---- clock radio

---- electric blanket/heater

---- electric broom

---- closet accessories

---- bathroom accessories
- scale
- guest towels
- decorative soap holder

---- spice set

---- candleholder/candles

---- stack tables

---- breakfast tray

---- portable freezer

---- kitchen accessories†

---- _____

---- _____

---- _____

---- _____

---- _____

## For the Home: Outdoor

---- weathervane

---- outdoor thermometer

---- birdhouse

---- hurricane lamp/insect lantern

---- sundial

---- patio furniture

---- swing/hammock

---- pool mattress

---- croquet set

---- badminton/volleyball set

---- lawn mower

---- garden equipment
- pruning shears
- tool tote
- windup hose

---- barbecue accessories††

---- picnic accessories
- cooler
- Thermos set

---- _____

---- _____

---- _____

---- _____

## Personal Items§

---- bathrobe/slippers

---- belt

*See "The Well-Stocked-Bar List," page 109.

†See "The Well-Equipped-Kitchen List," page 98.

††See "Informal Party Checklist," page 110.

§See "List of Basic Gifts for Children," page 143.

___ gloves

___ boots

___ hat/cap

___ shirt/blouse

___ handkerchiefs

___ fur jacket

___ vest

___ suspenders

___ lingerie

___ muffler/stole

___ scarf/ties

___ sweater

___ _____

___ _____

___ eyeglass-repair kit

___ jewelry

   • watch

   • ring

   • cufflinks/tie pin

   • bracelet/earrings

___ jewelry box

___ keyring

___ wallet

___ purse

___ credit-card holder

___ pipe/tobacco pouch/
   humidifier

___ lighter

___ toiletries

___ makeup mirror

___ framed photograph

___ photo album

___ penny bank

___ gift certificate

___ stocks/bonds

___ desk accessories

   • calendar

   • diary/address book

   • letter opener/holder

   • paperweight

   • pencil holder/sharpener

   • postage meter

___ wastebasket

___ stationery

___ calculator

___ _____

___ _____

## Special Interests*

___ pet accessories

___ camera/case

___ tools/tool box

___ power tools

___ gourmet goodies/tin delicacies

___ host/hostess apron/mitt

___ travel accessories

   • language/car cassettes

   • cosmetic case

   • car jumper cable

   • car vacuum

   • luggage/carrier

   • passport case

   • set of maps

*See "The Ultimate Hobby List," page 183.

___ bicycle

___ bowling ball

___ camping gear†

___ art supplies

___ portable loom

___ sewing machine

___ sewing basket

___ magnifying glass

___ metal detector

___ puzzles/board games

___ concert/sports/theater
   tickets

___ opera glasses/binoculars

___ museum membership

___ periodical subscription

___ _____

___ _____

___ _____

## Personal Service IOU's

___ homemade/hand-crafted
   items

___ do household repairs/
   carpentry

___ baby-/house-/pet-sit

___ paint/wallpaper a room

___ give free craft lessons

___ night on the town

___ tankful of gas

___ _____

___ _____

___ _____

†See "Outdoor Camping List," page 22.

# ✓ Gift Giver's Holiday Checklist

**Relatives**

___ spouse
___ mother
___ father
___ mother-in-law
___ father-in-law
___ son(s)-in-law
___ _____
___ daughter(s)-in-law
___ _____
___ brother(s)-in-law
___ _____
___ sister(s)-in-law
___ _____
___ grandmother(s)
___ _____
___ grandfather(s)
___ _____
___ grandchildren
___ _____
___ _____
___ _____
___ niece(s)
___ _____
___ _____
___ _____
___ nephew(s)
___ _____

___ _____
___ aunt(s)
___ _____
___ _____
___ uncle(s)
___ _____
___ _____
___ _____
___ cousin(s)
___ _____
___ _____
___ godparents
___ godchildren
___ other
___ _____

**Business Associates**

___ colleagues
___ _____
___ receptionist
___ secretary
___ office manager
___ boss
___ mail personnel
___ _____
___ clients/customers

___ _____
___ _____
___ _____
___ club affiliations
___ _____
___ banking/ financial personnel
___ _____
___ garage/parking
___ office cleaning help
___ _____

**Social Obligations**

___ neighbors
___ _____
___ _____
___ school personnel
___ _____
___ _____
___ classmates
___ _____
___ religious groups
___ clergypersons
___ friends
___ _____
___ _____
___ _____
___ club associates

___ philanthropic

**Apartment/House Workers**

___ housekeeper/nurse
___ apartment-house super
___ porters
___ _____
___ doormen
___ post-office workers
___ newspaper delivery people
___ handymen
___ _____
___ plumber
___ gardener
___ sanitation workers
___ _____
___ garage attendants
___ _____
___ car mechanic
___ _____
___ _____

# ✔ The Ultimate Hobby List

## The Arts

### Dancing
—— ballet

—— ballroom

—— disco

—— folk

—— jazz

—— square

—— tap

### Music
—— composing

—— guitar

—— piano

—— recorder

—— singing

—— band playing

—— orchestra

—— rock/chamber group

### Drama
—— acting

—— stagecraft

—— mime

—— puppetry

—— ventriloquism

—— writing

### Arts and Crafts
—— basketry

—— batik

—— beadcraft

—— bookbinding

—— calligraphy

—— candlemaking

—— cartooning

—— ceramics

—— clay modeling

—— crocheting

—— decoupage

—— drawing

—— embroidery

—— enameling

—— gem cutting/polishing

—— glass etching

—— jewelrymaking

—— kitecraft

—— knitting

—— latch-hooking

—— leathercraft

—— macrame

—— mobiles

—— mosaics

—— moviemaking/animation

—— needlepoint

—— origami

—— painting

—— patchwork

—— photography

—— printing

—— quilting

—— sculpture

—— sewing

—— soap carving

—— weaving

—— whittling

—— wirecraft

—— wood carving/woodcuts

—— ——————

—— ——————

—— ——————

## Nature/Animals

—— backpacking

—— camping

—— mountaineering

—— birdwatching

—— orienteering

—— gardening

—— flower arranging

—— beekeeping

—— dog breeding

—— tropical fish

—— ——————

—— ——————

—— ——————

## Science/Electronics

—— archeology

—— astronomy

—— meteorology

—— rocketry

—— modelmaking

—— ham radio

—— chemistry

—— computers

—— ——————

—— ——————

—— ——————

## Do-It-Yourself

—— home repairs

—— car tinkering

—— refinishing furniture

—— winemaking

—— preserving

—— baking

—— cooking

—— ——————

—— ——————

## Sports

—— archery

—— baseball

—— basketball

—— bicycling

—— boating

—— bowling

—— canoeing

—— fencing

—— fishing

—— flying

___ golf

___ gymnastics

___ hiking

___ hockey

___ horseback riding

___ hunting

___ ice skating

___ judo/karate

___ roller skating

___ running

___ sailing

___ skin diving

___ skiing

___ snorkeling

___ soccer

___ squash

___ surfing

___ swimming

___ tennis

___ volleyball

___ water skiing

___ _____

___ _____

**Games**

___ astrology

___ backgammon

___ bridge

___ chess

___ magic

___ _____

___ _____

**Collecting**

___ advertising give-aways

___ antique cars

___ arrowheads

___ art

___ art glass

___ autographs

___ baseball cards

___ baskets

___ bells

___ books

___ bottles

___ boxes

___ butterflies

___ buttons

___ cigar bands

___ clocks

___ coins

___ comics

___ decoys

___ dolls

___ dollhouses

___ doorstops

___ fans

___ gems

___ guns

___ insects

___ jazz memorabilia

___ locks

___ marbles

___ match covers

___ medals

___ menus

___ miniatures

___ molds

___ neon signs

___ paperweights

___ pewter

___ playing cards

___ postcards

___ posters

___ prints

___ quilts

___ recipes

___ samplers

___ scrimshaw

___ shells

___ sheet music

___ silver

___ spoons

___ stamps

___ tin containers

___ tools

___ toy banks

___ train models

___ tree ornaments

___ weathervanes

___ windup toys

___ _____

___ _____

___ _____

___ _____

___ _____

# ✔ Things to Do When Wallet/Purse Is Lost

- ___ paycheck
- ___ house keys
- ___ office keys
- ___ car keys
- ___ safe-deposit-box key
- ___ cash
- ___ locker key
- ___ sunglasses
- ___ glasses
- ___ telephone/address book
- ___ business cards

- ___ credit/charge cards
- ___ check-cashing card
- ___ checkbook
- ___ loose blank checks
- ___ savings passbook
- ___ traveler's checks
- ___ driver's license
- ___ car registration
- ___ wallet
- ___ journal
- ___ photos
- ___ lists

- ___ appointment dates
- ___ social security card
- ___ medical insurance I.D.
- ___ passport
- ___ library card
- ___ prescriptions
- ___ letters
- ___ bills
- ___ jewelry/watch
- ___ membership cards

- ___ plane tickets
- ___ theater tickets
- ___ cleaning/repair tickets
- ___ stamps
- ___ receipts
- ___ _____
- ___ _____
- ___ _____
- ___ _____

- Check itemized list above.
- Alert boss to notify bank. If paycheck is cashed with forged signature, the amount must be credited to your boss's account; you get replacement check.
- Report to local precinct; note date, case claim number for insurance purposes.
- Call insurance company to check coverage, request claim form.
- Notify credit-card issuers immediately. You are not liable for any unauthorized charges made after you report the loss or theft.
- Notify banks; they will put savings accounts on hold until you sign lost passbook affidavit; by providing numbers on missing checks you may avoid closing out account.
- Arrange for locksmith to change locks.
- Bring proof of signature and car insurance to the Department of Motor Vehicles for immediate license and car registration duplicate.
- Report missing traveler's checks to original issuer.

- Register loss with airline that issued ticket; fill out lost-ticket form. (You are not protected if someone uses or cashes in your ticket before written form is processed.)
- Inform Passport Office or Embassy of loss.
- Inform all organizations of loss of your membership cards (library, etc.).
- Call any social security office to apply for duplicate card; you are required to present two original I.D. documents.
- Contact repair shops/cleaners/druggist about loss.
- Call doctors/dentist/lawyer about any appointments in the near future; reconfirm time, date.
- Notify business firms for any duplicate bills needed.
- Replace other items checked off on list.
- _____
- _____

# ✓ Things to Consider Before Remarrying

- Do you/prospective spouse know one another's outlook on:

  ____ adopting stepchildren

  ____ childrearing

  ____ religious differences

  ____ dual-career household

  ____ future plans (for a family/life style/retirement)

  ____ type of wedding reception

  ____ _____

  ____ _____

- Are you clear about living arrangements?

  ____ where you will live (his/her/new place)

  ____ what furnishings you will integrate/place in storage/dispose of

  ____ space requirements for children of previous marriage

  ____ who will take authority of children/ under what circumstances

  ____ visitation rights (if other parent has custody)

  ____ room arrangements

  ____ ground rules during visits

  ____ _____

  ____ _____

- Do you know each other's financial situation? Have you figured out how remarriage may affect:

  ____ your income/benefits

  ____ expenses

____ prior commitments on maintenance/alimony

____ child support

____ outstanding debts/investments

____ _____

____ _____

- Have you discussed legal matters? Will you need to make decisions regarding:

  ____ premarital agreement (what it covers/for how long)

  ____ ownership of assets (now and for the future)

  - bank accounts/safe-deposit box

  - real estate

  ____ joint or individual credit/charge cards

  ____ beneficiaries named on personal insurance/ employee benefits

  ____ wills/changes you plan to make

  ____ use of a former name

  ____ _____

  ____ _____

- Who needs to be notified about changes in name/status/address?

  ____ social security office

  ____ IRS

  ____ Department of Motor Vehicles

  ____ store/credit offices/banks

  ____ professional/business associations

  ____ landlord/condo/co-op board

  ____ _____

# ✔ Personal Safety Checklist

## In Dangerous Situations

☐ If you feel you are being followed:

___ cross the street

___ avoid going straight home

___ walk faster to nearest store/gas station and call the police

___ run into nearest public telephone booth, brace yourself against the closed door and dial for help

☐ If held up:

___ talk in a soft voice and stay calm

___ give up property rather than resist

___ try to note identifying marks/traits

___ fight only if your life is in danger

___ report incident to police immediately

☐ If your life is threatened in an attack:

___ scream and run

___ gouge attacker's eyes with your thumbs

___ kick shins/bend fingers back/jab knee into groin

☐ If followed into an elevator:

___ pretend to have forgotten something and get out

___ stand near panel ready to push emergency or several floor buttons

___ yell "Fire" not "Help" if attack appears imminent

## On the Street

___ walk with a confident manner

___ avoid doorways and shortcuts

___ walk with someone at night

___ carry flashlight/whistle or Freon horn in hand when alone

___ reject rides from all strangers

___ walk in opposite direction of car when harassed by its passengers

## In Public Areas

___ vary your routine tasks at night (laundromat)

___ avoid using public restroom

___ avoid sitting alone in movie

___ avoid announcing your name/address in public

___ avoid using computerized banking at night

## At Home

___ ask taxi driver to wait until you are inside

___ check elevator mirror for person hidden in corner

___ ring buzzer when coming back to empty house to scare off intruder

___ call police from outside when you see signs of break-in

___ refuse to open front door for strangers

___ make emergency call for stranger who asks to use phone

___ call to verify I.D. before letting in utility/repair person

# ✔ Your Official Numbers List

—————————social security number

—————————car registration

—————————car license

—————————driver's license

—————————hospital health insurance

—————————car insurance

—————————homeowner's insurance

—————————life insurance

—————————credit cards

—————————

—————————

—————————

—————————

—————————department store charge cards

—————————

—————————

—————————

—————————

—————————AAA policy

—————————

—————————

—————————

—————————

—————————

# ✓ List of Important Dates for Your Calendar

Remember to note on datebook beginning of new year

## Financial due dates

___ mortgage payments

___ personal loans

___ car loan

___ school tuition(s)

___ income tax

___ investments/dividends

___ insurance premiums

___ _____

___ _____

___ _____

## Renewal/expiration dates

___ credit cards

___ insurance policies

___ memberships

___ car inspection/registration

___ driver's license

___ library card

___ _____

___ _____

___ _____

## Applications

___ school/college

___ camp

___ campsites

___ medicare

___ membership organizations

___ _____

___ _____

## School-related

___ vacations

___ conferences

___ special classes

___ graduations

___ class reunions

___ _____

___ _____

## Personal

___ birthdays

___ anniversaries

___ memorial service

___ religious observances

___ family reunion

___ vacations

___ health checkups (dental/ eye/immunizations)

___ social events

___ business trips

___ special meetings

___ salary review

___ holidays

___ _____

___ _____

___ _____

# Your Personal Checklist

1   **When You Travel**

2   **At Work**

3   **Where You Live**

4   **Your Finances and Records**

5   **Keeping Your Home in Shape**

6   **Your Household**

7   **Your Car**

8   **Your Children**

9   **Your Health**

# When You Travel

- [ ] _____
- [ ] _____
- [ ] _____
- [ ] _____
- [ ] _____
- [ ] _____
- [ ] _____
- [ ] _____
- [ ] _____
- [ ] _____
- [ ] _____
- [ ] _____
- [ ] _____
- [ ] _____
- [ ] _____
- [ ] _____
- [ ] _____
- [ ] _____
- [ ] _____
- [ ] _____
- [ ] _____
- [ ] _____

- [ ] _____
- [ ] _____
- [ ] _____
- [ ] _____
- [ ] _____
- [ ] _____
- [ ] _____
- [ ] _____
- [ ] _____
- [ ] _____
- [ ] _____
- [ ] _____
- [ ] _____
- [ ] _____
- [ ] _____
- [ ] _____
- [ ] _____
- [ ] _____
- [ ] _____
- [ ] _____
- [ ] _____
- [ ] _____

# When You Travel

# At Work

- [ ] _____
- [ ] _____
- [ ] _____
- [ ] _____
- [ ] _____
- [ ] _____
- [ ] _____
- [ ] _____
- [ ] _____
- [ ] _____
- [ ] _____
- [ ] _____
- [ ] _____
- [ ] _____
- [ ] _____
- [ ] _____
- [ ] _____
- [ ] _____
- [ ] _____
- [ ] _____
- [ ] _____

- [ ] _____
- [ ] _____
- [ ] _____
- [ ] _____
- [ ] _____
- [ ] _____
- [ ] _____
- [ ] _____
- [ ] _____
- [ ] _____
- [ ] _____
- [ ] _____
- [ ] _____
- [ ] _____
- [ ] _____
- [ ] _____
- [ ] _____
- [ ] _____
- [ ] _____
- [ ] _____
- [ ] _____

# At Work

- ☐ _____
- ☐ _____
- ☐ _____
- ☐ _____
- ☐ _____
- ☐ _____
- ☐ _____
- ☐ _____
- ☐ _____
- ☐ _____
- ☐ _____
- ☐ _____
- ☐ _____
- ☐ _____
- ☐ _____
- ☐ _____
- ☐ _____
- ☐ _____
- ☐ _____
- ☐ _____
- ☐ _____
- ☐ _____
- ☐ _____

- ☐ _____
- ☐ _____
- ☐ _____
- ☐ _____
- ☐ _____
- ☐ _____
- ☐ _____
- ☐ _____
- ☐ _____
- ☐ _____
- ☐ _____
- ☐ _____
- ☐ _____
- ☐ _____
- ☐ _____
- ☐ _____
- ☐ _____
- ☐ _____
- ☐ _____
- ☐ _____
- ☐ _____
- ☐ _____
- ☐ _____

# Where You Live

☐ _____    ☐ _____
☐ _____    ☐ _____
☐ _____    ☐ _____
☐ _____    ☐ _____
☐ _____    ☐ _____
☐ _____    ☐ _____
☐ _____    ☐ _____
☐ _____    ☐ _____
☐ _____    ☐ _____
☐ _____    ☐ _____
☐ _____    ☐ _____
☐ _____    ☐ _____
☐ _____    ☐ _____
☐ _____    ☐ _____
☐ _____    ☐ _____
☐ _____    ☐ _____
☐ _____    ☐ _____
☐ _____    ☐ _____
☐ _____    ☐ _____
☐ _____    ☐ _____
☐ _____    ☐ _____

# Where You Live

☐ _____    ☐ _____
☐ _____    ☐ _____
☐ _____    ☐ _____
☐ _____    ☐ _____
☐ _____    ☐ _____
☐ _____    ☐ _____
☐ _____    ☐ _____
☐ _____    ☐ _____
☐ _____    ☐ _____
☐ _____    ☐ _____
☐ _____    ☐ _____
☐ _____    ☐ _____
☐ _____    ☐ _____
☐ _____    ☐ _____
☐ _____    ☐ _____
☐ _____    ☐ _____
☐ _____    ☐ _____
☐ _____    ☐ _____
☐ _____    ☐ _____
☐ _____    ☐ _____
☐ _____    ☐ _____
☐ _____    ☐ _____

# Your Finances and Records

- [ ] _____
- [ ] _____
- [ ] _____
- [ ] _____
- [ ] _____
- [ ] _____
- [ ] _____
- [ ] _____
- [ ] _____
- [ ] _____
- [ ] _____
- [ ] _____
- [ ] _____
- [ ] _____
- [ ] _____
- [ ] _____
- [ ] _____
- [ ] _____
- [ ] _____
- [ ] _____
- [ ] _____

- [ ] _____
- [ ] _____
- [ ] _____
- [ ] _____
- [ ] _____
- [ ] _____
- [ ] _____
- [ ] _____
- [ ] _____
- [ ] _____
- [ ] _____
- [ ] _____
- [ ] _____
- [ ] _____
- [ ] _____
- [ ] _____
- [ ] _____
- [ ] _____
- [ ] _____
- [ ] _____
- [ ] _____

# Your Finances and Records

☐ _____     ☐ _____

☐ _____     ☐ _____

☐ _____     ☐ _____

☐ _____     ☐ _____

☐ _____     ☐ _____

☐ _____     ☐ _____

☐ _____     ☐ _____

☐ _____     ☐ _____

☐ _____     ☐ _____

☐ _____     ☐ _____

☐ _____     ☐ _____

☐ _____     ☐ _____

☐ _____     ☐ _____

☐ _____     ☐ _____

☐ _____     ☐ _____

☐ _____     ☐ _____

☐ _____     ☐ _____

☐ _____     ☐ _____

☐ _____     ☐ _____

☐ _____     ☐ _____

☐ _____     ☐ _____

# Keeping Your Home in Shape

☐ _____

☐ _____

☐ _____

☐ _____

☐ _____

☐ _____

☐ _____

☐ _____

☐ _____

☐ _____

☐ _____

☐ _____

☐ _____

☐ _____

☐ _____

☐ _____

☐ _____

☐ _____

☐ _____

☐ _____

☐ _____

☐ _____

☐ _____

☐ _____

☐ _____

☐ _____

☐ _____

☐ _____

☐ _____

☐ _____

☐ _____

☐ _____

☐ _____

☐ _____

☐ _____

☐ _____

☐ _____

☐ _____

☐ _____

☐ _____

☐ _____

☐ _____

# Your Household

☐ _____     ☐ _____
☐ _____     ☐ _____
☐ _____     ☐ _____
☐ _____     ☐ _____
☐ _____     ☐ _____
☐ _____     ☐ _____
☐ _____     ☐ _____
☐ _____     ☐ _____
☐ _____     ☐ _____
☐ _____     ☐ _____
☐ _____     ☐ _____
☐ _____     ☐ _____
☐ _____     ☐ _____
☐ _____     ☐ _____
☐ _____     ☐ _____
☐ _____     ☐ _____
☐ _____     ☐ _____
☐ _____     ☐ _____
☐ _____     ☐ _____
☐ _____     ☐ _____
☐ _____     ☐ _____

# Your Car

☐ _____
☐ _____
☐ _____
☐ _____
☐ _____
☐ _____
☐ _____
☐ _____
☐ _____
☐ _____
☐ _____
☐ _____
☐ _____
☐ _____
☐ _____
☐ _____
☐ _____
☐ _____
☐ _____
☐ _____
☐ _____
☐ _____

☐ _____
☐ _____
☐ _____
☐ _____
☐ _____
☐ _____
☐ _____
☐ _____
☐ _____
☐ _____
☐ _____
☐ _____
☐ _____
☐ _____
☐ _____
☐ _____
☐ _____
☐ _____
☐ _____
☐ _____
☐ _____
☐ _____

# Your Car

# Your Children

- ☐ _____
- ☐ _____
- ☐ _____
- ☐ _____
- ☐ _____
- ☐ _____
- ☐ _____
- ☐ _____
- ☐ _____
- ☐ _____
- ☐ _____
- ☐ _____
- ☐ _____
- ☐ _____
- ☐ _____
- ☐ _____
- ☐ _____
- ☐ _____
- ☐ _____
- ☐ _____
- ☐ _____

- ☐ _____
- ☐ _____
- ☐ _____
- ☐ _____
- ☐ _____
- ☐ _____
- ☐ _____
- ☐ _____
- ☐ _____
- ☐ _____
- ☐ _____
- ☐ _____
- ☐ _____
- ☐ _____
- ☐ _____
- ☐ _____
- ☐ _____
- ☐ _____
- ☐ _____
- ☐ _____
- ☐ _____

# Your Children

☐ _____     ☐ _____

☐ _____     ☐ _____

☐ _____     ☐ _____

☐ _____     ☐ _____

☐ _____     ☐ _____

☐ _____     ☐ _____

☐ _____     ☐ _____

☐ _____     ☐ _____

☐ _____     ☐ _____

☐ _____     ☐ _____

☐ _____     ☐ _____

☐ _____     ☐ _____

☐ _____     ☐ _____

☐ _____     ☐ _____

☐ _____     ☐ _____

☐ _____     ☐ _____

☐ _____     ☐ _____

☐ _____     ☐ _____

☐ _____     ☐ _____

☐ _____     ☐ _____

☐ _____     ☐ _____

# Your Health

☐ _____    ☐ _____

☐ _____    ☐ _____

☐ _____    ☐ _____

☐ _____    ☐ _____

☐ _____    ☐ _____

☐ _____    ☐ _____

☐ _____    ☐ _____

☐ _____    ☐ _____

☐ _____    ☐ _____

☐ _____    ☐ _____

☐ _____    ☐ _____

☐ _____    ☐ _____

☐ _____    ☐ _____

☐ _____    ☐ _____

☐ _____    ☐ _____

☐ _____    ☐ _____

☐ _____    ☐ _____

☐ _____    ☐ _____

☐ _____    ☐ _____

☐ _____    ☐ _____

☐ _____    ☐ _____

☐ _____    ☐ _____

☐ _____    ☐ _____

# Your Health

□ _____   □ _____
□ _____   □ _____
□ _____   □ _____
□ _____   □ _____
□ _____   □ _____
□ _____   □ _____
□ _____   □ _____
□ _____   □ _____
□ _____   □ _____
□ _____   □ _____
□ _____   □ _____
□ _____   □ _____
□ _____   □ _____
□ _____   □ _____
□ _____   □ _____
□ _____   □ _____
□ _____   □ _____
□ _____   □ _____
□ _____   □ _____
□ _____   □ _____
□ _____   □ _____

# Index